HOLOBALL

A PITTSBURGH MURDER MYSTERY

TOM RINKES

Copyright © 2021 Tom Rinkes

All rights reserved. No part of this book may be reproduced, stored, or transmitted by any means—whether auditory, graphic, mechanical, or electronic—without written permission of both publisher and author, except in the case of brief excerpts used in critical articles and reviews. Unauthorized reproduction of any part of this work is illegal and is punishable by law.

ISBN: 978-1-949735-52-9 (sc)
ISBN: 978-1-949735-54-3 (hc)
ISBN: 978-1-949735-55-0 (e)

Because of the dynamic nature of the Internet, any web addresses or links contained in this book may have changed since publication and may no longer be valid. The views expressed in this work are solely those of the author and do not necessarily reflect the views of the publisher, and the publisher hereby disclaims any responsibility for them.

The Ewings Publishing LLC
One Galleria Blvd., Suite 1900, Metairie, LA 70001
1-888-421-2397

CONTENTS

Chapter 1	Franco and Steak Fries	1
Chapter 2	To The Call	6
Chapter 3	The Screamer	12
Chapter 4	Pending Consultations	18
Chapter 5	Ashes of Evidence	23
Chapter 6	Booze, Lies and Plaster Tales	42
Chapter 7	Who is Here?	48
Chapter 8	Fun in Germantown	55
Chapter 9	The Succer Bowl	69
Chapter 10	Money Talks, the Other Stuff Walks	76
Chapter 11	The Play	82

CHAPTER ONE

FRANCO AND STEAK FRIES

"Is this for real?" my partner asked.

"Yeah," I said as I raised my empty glass for a refill. "It's as real as you and I sitting here watching it."

"Did your brother really invent this?" he asked.

"That's what he says, but I'll still don't know how to check my email right, so who am I to doubt?"

It was Saturday night, the twenty-third of December, 1995 when my partner Vinnie and I sat to celebrate the twenty-first anniversary of the Immaculate Reception, which almost put our team in a Super Bowl. Our choice of watering holes this night was Club 40, an abandoned warehouse turned night club at the far south end of the Strip District in Pittsburgh, Pennsylvania. It was clandestine, it was a cool place and the second floor was **very** pricy. On the ceiling was this thing I called a contraption about ten feet long and six wide. The all-black metal frame was dotted with small, oval holes every foot or so to let the heat out while multi-colored lights flashed on it everywhere. The first time I saw it I thought I was watching a rerun of that Close Encounters of the Third Kind flic, but what impressed me the most was the guys on the floor.

My younger and only brother, Albert, along with another computer genius who wants to remain anonymous, had invented a way to watch a football game in a room about a hundred feet long and half as wide. All the players were about a foot tall but proportionate to their body size and were—now get this—holograms. Albert calls his gizmo "HoloBall" but he's yet to apply for a patent, for IRS reasons I'm sure. The cost of a Friday night ticket to witness this miracle of technology was a thousand dollars a pop, cash only. The mock stadium, that was a replica of Three Rivers, held forty guests, hence the name Club 40. All beverages were on the house, as was mine and Vinnie's tickets, because there were certain "officials" who needed their palms greased so that the NFL people didn't find out and want their cut and we were just the people to do it diplomatically, so to speak.

With my third scotch-n-soda in hand I moved closer to the game. A play was coming up and I wanted to prove something to Vinnie once and for all.

"Hey Vin," I yelled. "Get over here and watch this. I'm gonna show you I'm right about this. It'll be in black and white…I mean gold."

Vincent Falbo was about six feet tall, lean, muscular and sported a head of greying hair that made toupee artists shudder. He was a street-hardened tough guy who didn't run to or from **nobody** and as he nonchalantly strolled over I got the greeting I knew I'd get.

"What, what—what do you want?" he barked.

"Bend down here and watch this last play—have you got your contacts in?"

"Yeah, but I still see what I want to see and what I don't, I don't."

With twenty-two seconds left in the Steelers' first playoff game, and Oakland leading 7-6, Coach Noll called a pass play; 66 circle something. Two hefty dudes names Jones and Cline were about to sack Terry Bradshaw, he threw the ball to "Frenchy" Fuqua who then was hit hard by some scumbag named Jack Tatum. The ball popped into the air, end over end, and Franco Harris allegedly caught it before it hit the ground and the rest is NFL history.

"Now," I yelled. "Did you see that, Vinnie? Franco didn't catch the ball; he picked it off the ground. What more can I say? I rest my case." And then I felt the effect of eight-four eyes—which included my bro—burning a hole in my unworthy soul. I was a born-n-bred Burg kid, and I'd just committed a sin so great that I could've gotten excommunicated for it. After realizing my lack of good judgment, I hung my head in shame.

"Now, Jacob Johnson," Vinnie said calmly after taking a two-second gulp of his Stroh's beer. "Allow me—and for your sake I hope this is the last time—to school you on what *I* saw. Franco Harris caught that ball fair and square—albeit three or maybe two millimeters off the grass—but that football never touched the green. But…if you're still not satisfied I tell you what. Let's get that ball from the Rooney's and we'll just do one of those Carbon 14 or 15 date tests on it. I'll even split the bill for it with you fifty-fifty. What I'm saying here is that I bet my **ass** there ain't no **grass** on that ball for that particular hour, minute and second that this so-called offense occurred. What say you, brainiac?"

I looked hard at the man who'd taught me everything I needed to know in my chosen profession. Vinnie was fifteen years my elder and at fifty he was a prize specimen at what he needed to know and handled himself with the confidence of a man who'd been there-done that more than once. I felt grateful that after passing the test to move up from beat cop to Detective in the Pittsburgh Police Department, he became my mentor in the division I'd always dreamed of.

That being, Homicide.

"I guess," I started as I tried to get the taste of crow out of my mouth, "that I'll go downstairs and talk to Yana. She's a whole lot friendlier than you, and better looking."

My sister-in-law ran the street level bar/restaurant, and little did I know that all my professional training would be tested in the next few days.

-2-

Yana Romanovna Johnson was the twenty-five year old daughter of Russian parents who found their way to East Germany in the late seventies. Her father did quite well with the Communist government mainly because of his only daughter's intellectual talent. She worked closely with the KGB, only because if she didn't her parents would suddenly vanish. After the Wall fell they made their way to the West side but her papa kept a tight lid on her capabilities so she could live a normal life void of the CIA. Yana, was something else.

She would park her very feminine, five-foot seven-inch frame at the barstool on the very end of the all-wooden counter. She had a crew of four Pitt college kids who worked for her and she was gracious enough, even though she took the orders, to let them have all the tips. Yana would have the customers seated and served menus. As the waiter poured their water glasses full they'd take a drink order. As the preliminaries were finished Yana studied everyone at the table intently. I mean she was zoned out. Then she'd take out her standard memo pad and assign them a number; as in one through six. Under each circled number was their order, and her accuracy rate on this was one hundred percent.

You see, this brown-eyed, high-cheeked bone Eastern Block beauty was the world's first, and maybe only, physic waitress.

As the servers laid the plates in front of the flabbergasted customers, the order was thus. Number one (father) had Veal Parmesan, salad with ranch dressing and a Budweiser—twenty-ounce—draught, number two (mother) had the Chef's Salad with a Bud Light back, in a chilled glass. Numbers three and four (boy and girl, both tweeners) smiled in delight with their double bacon cheeseburger, steak fries on the side, a large, Coke Classic in a very tall glass and strawed up to boot. Number five (grandma) seemed content with her big bowl of homemade vegetable soup, Ritz crackers around the plate. Number five (grandpa) looked pretty much pissed off about everything and just stared at his grilled cheese, cole slaw and tall water. Yana could work miracles, but she has to have something to work with, and Gramps appeared arthritic, irritable and looking like he was in dire need of the nearest Men's Room.

Eventually the six table-fourteen-booth mini restaurant was filled, with people waiting in line, sometimes even outside. The bar held the usual counter-creeps—including moi—that came in steadily each night to drink the night away, talk football and the like. I especially liked to sit at the back end—but never in Yana's seat; that would be a sacrilege—and watch her work her magic. Albert was lucky enough to meet her while working for the Pentagon in Berlin after the Fall, doing whatever the Steve Job types do. He was the brains in the family and I was still looking for the "Relete" button on my computer to try to get back all that I'd lost.

As the party of three was waiting their turn I spied some old dude starring a hole in Yana. Everywhere she went so did those beady blue eyes of his. I kept watching Yana to see if she'd pick up on that and then she slowly—like she really didn't want to—turned and eyeballed the guy. He fled out the door, leaving his party trailing after him. He didn't come back in that night and I stayed till closing time to make sure she'd be alright. There was something about him that bothered me, and Yana lost a step or two in her usually hurried gate that night I swear because of him.

Yet, maybe he just wasn't in the mood for grilled cheese.

CHAPTER TWO

TO THE CALL

The night went smoothly after that with upstairs and downstairs customers coming and going at their will and whim. Another game was started up top and I knew Vinnie had had enough to drink when I heard him yell, "**Tackle that sonofabitch, why don't you!?**" three or four times. I was nursing my fourth—and last—scotch when Tommy "The Hack" McGuire walked in. He was short, stout with a black tee-shirt that covered eighty-five per cent of his Iron City belly and chomping on a DeNobli cigar. His gray, golfer's cap was on a little crooked and leaning to the left as per most men...I mean the hat. He offered his services as the only independent cab driver on this side of the Allegheny who took drunks home for a cut rate. He was mine and Vin's steady designated driver on heavy drinking nights such as this, and in return I'd slip him some very good tips on the best horse to bet a Jackson ($20 bill) or two on with his bookie this coming Friday night.

I'm not a dirty cop per se, but I strive to see people I like be in the "Happy Room", and I'm not above showing them what could be behind Door Number One.

As Yana was helping her crew clean up the tables after the last customer left I noticed she'd wipe a table with her usual white tornado, circular swift-and-sure motion that made most crumbs wish they'd been eaten, if they could feel pain, that is. But, now she would swipe...and look up... swipe some more and look at the wall. Something was bugging her and seeing as how Albert was up there counting his thousands, I felt it my duty to investigate.

And before I go any further I've got to tell you the reader that I was deadly, and secretly, in love with this woman and had been since Al brought her here from Germany with a ring on her left hand, which means she's off limits.

But she's psychic, and the lady already knows that. I approached her using the nickname I gave her once.

"Yana Svetlana, what's the problem?" I asked sympathetically.

"Come, let us sit at the bar. I need coffee. Would you, pretty please?"

As I walked around the business end of the bar—and knowing she had my number big time—I poured one black for me and a light-n-sweet for her. We sat, took a gulp, and then she spoke.

"I do not know, Jacob, but a man who was here earlier—how should I say this—has...unwinded me?"

"You mean he unwound you?"

"Yes, that is what I meant. I received many bad...gyrations...from him."

"You mean vibrations?"

"You Americana's talk so funny."

"Tell me about it. What man was it?"

"He was elderly, and came in with two women. When I was doing...my...how do you say?"

"Your thing?"

"Yes, yes, that is it. It was as if he stare a hole in the back of my back."

I'll let Gorbachev figure that one out, I thought.

"What was it about him? Didn't he know what he wanted to eat?"

"Oh, no; he **was** hungry. He was...perplexed...and sad...and very angry too. I have never been wary of someone's thoughts but this man was...dark...and sinister and had done much violence in his life. I became—for one of your split seconds—afraid."

Her eyes dropped to the bar as she cleaned it. She grew strangely quiet which was so unlike her. I **did** carry a gun and had dealt with some bad dudes in my career, so I wasn't sweatin' it. Yet, she needed a little comfort.

"My dear, don't worry about it. As far as this guy—or anyone else—giving you any gruff, it ain't happening."

That seemed to comfort her. All of a sudden I heard a round of boisterous laughter coming from the "Game Room" and knew Vinnie had started his comedy audition.

I never missed one of his performances because he knew some five-star jokes.

-2-

Vinnie was a friendly enough guy unless you rubbed him the wrong way. He stood at the south end of the stadium, cigar in one hand and a now mixed drink in the other, smiling as was everyone around him. He could mesmerize a crowd, an interviewee, a known felon or someone who was just, as he put it, a PIMA (Pain In My Ass). He was "holding court" as any master story teller could do. He began with one I'd heard several times.

"There was this Italian barber, Donny, who was trimming his nephew, Franky. Donny asked him where he and the misses were going on vacation.

'We're going to Italy, Uncle Don. Have you ever been there?' Franky asked.

'Yea, I was there once. What part you going too?'

'Rome. Ever been there?'

'Let me tell you what, sonny. You **don't** want to go there.'

'Why not?' Franky asked.

'Cause, it smells like sewage and there's pick pockets everywhere.'

'Well, we already got the tickets bought.'

Now Franky thought that was the end of that, but he shoulda known better.

'Ok, ok. What airline you gonna use?' Donny asked.

'Delta'.

'**Delta!?** Delta sucks. If you even get a meal it'll be cold.'

'Well, that's what the travel agent set us up with.'

'Alright, okay. What you and the wife gonna do when you get there?'

'We got an audience with the Pope,' Franky said proudly.

'Audience my **ass**! You'll be about a mile away and the Pope'll look about two inches high. I feel for ya'.'

So Franky goes home feeling lower than whale shit, but keeps it to himself and they leave. Two months later he went back for a trim. He sat in the chair without speaking to his uncle, waiting for him to draw first blood.

'Well, did you go to Rome, my boy?'

'Yes we did.'

'Stunk, didn't it?'

'No, it didn't. I don't know where you stayed, but where we were at all I could smell was linguini sauce and roses. In fact, I kept my wallet in my back pocket for two weeks and nobody made a move on it.'

Score Franky 1 Donny 0.

"Yeah? But how 'bout the flight over. You come back starving?' Donny asked.

'No. to tell the truth we had two hots on the way over and two on the way back. The food was excellent.'

Score Franky 2-zip.

Now Donny was getting a little peeved at what used to be his favorite nephew. 'Ok, wise guy, did you get your audience with the Pontiff?'

'Why yes we did. I even stood right beside him and shook his hand.'

This impressed the barber so much he walked around to the front of the chair with a look of amazement on his clean-shaven face. '**Really? No kiddin'?** What did he say?'

'Awh, nothing much. He just looked up at me and asked,

'Where on earth did you get that shitty-lookin' haircut?'

Donny was three and out, and Franky never went around his uncle again when he was holding anything with a sharp edge. I'm done."

I looked at the clock and tapped my partner on the shoulder.

"C'mon, Vin. We're done here. We've got to get some sleep."

I helped the now drunk man down the steps, signaled for Tommy to pull out front and almost poured Vinnie into the back seat. As I was putting his hat over his eyes I looked across the street and the old geezer that spooked Yana was pacing up and down. I yelled "STOP" and that shook Vinnie up. He tried to get out of the cab to "answer the call" but started to slide out and by the time I caught him and put him back the mystery fossil was gone. I had one of those gut feelings that cops get.

I *will* see this dude again.

-3-

The ride to Bloomfield took about ten minutes at this hour of the morning. Vinnie and I both lived off Friendship Avenue; he on the main drag and I up Coral Street. As soon as we stopped in front of his house, the porch light came on and the front door started to open.

"Oh shit," Tommy said. "Branna's up."

Branna Falbo was Vinnie's Irish-American wife of twenty years and once Vin told me her name was Gaelic for "a beauty with hair as black as a raven's eye" and that she was. In her late thirties, I'm guessing, she came henceforth at full speed with her long, flowered house coat whipping in the breeze she created. On nights like this her dark, brown eyes were almost black and mean looking. Even her all-natural Maybelline eyelashes couldn't sweeten up the look she gave me. I knew I was in for an old-fashioned ass-chewing.

"*Johnson!*" she yelled as she drug her husband out of the cab. "I told you a hundred times to keep my man outta that bar of your worthless brother. I oughta make you come in and pull him into bed. You think I enjoy this? He only gets this way when he's with you—what are you smiling about!?"

"I was just thinking, Mrs. Falbo, that I'd do that for you, but do I have to tuck him in too?"

I made this wise crack while I was still in the cab, because my mom didn't raise no fool, and there was no way I was going to chance her taking a swing at me. Then Tommy started to chuckle and that caused me to have one of those biting-a-hole-in-my-lip-to-keep-from-cracking up kind of smiles. She propped Vinnie up against the tall hedges around their place and stuck her whole head inside the back window.

"Jacob," she said calmly. "One of these days I'm gonna hire some wrangler to kick your ass proper. You understand what I'm saying here, smart guy?"

"Yes, ma'am, I do, and top of the morning to you. Tell your husband I'll see him Tuesday."

I didn't have to motion for Tommy to mash his gas and get me out of there because he knew the drill. I walked up the outside steps to my humble abode and crashed. With no woman in my life just then, I decided to spend Christmas Day by my lonesome.

-4-

At ten a.m. sharp Tuesday morning I found Vinnie at his desk, looking primed, trimmed and typing a report. You'd never know the man was blitzed two days back by the attention he gave his work. He was a good cop and demanded nothing less than my best at every assignment given us. This week's one was especially grisly.

"Jake, look this over while I snatch a coffee. It's ugly."

"The coffee?" I asked.

"No, the case. What'd you do this morning, take a dumbass pill or something?"

I chuckled, let that one go and did my job. A Pitt student—female, blonde, Caucasian, age twenty-two—had been on the bike trail in town early Sunday morning when a man grabbed, raped and strangled her, leaving her broken body in the bushes. I sat and starred at her autopsy pics in disbelief, as I did all senseless murders.

My Lord, I thought. *What could she possibly have done to deserve this? It's time to live up to our motto.*

Vinnie and I are Homicide Cops, and we speak for the dead. That's our mission in life.

"Vinnie," I said as he sat back down and took a sip. "Where you want to start on this one?"

"Up and down Seventh Street. There's a whole bunch of those fancy-smanchy new apartments there with doormen and the like always outside. Maybe one of them saw or heard something. I don't know, but it's worth a shot."

I was chompin' at the bit to start this one. For some unknown reason—another gut feeling maybe?—I knew this case would be special.

CHAPTER THREE

THE SCREAMER

1995 was the beginning of the Pittsburgh "Renaissance" period where many abandoned office buildings and dilapidated storefronts were being retrofitted with high-rise apartments and trendy shops. The bicycle craze had hit the downtown area, with numerous bike lanes running perpendicular to streets like the 7th. Many of the trails were along the river fronts, neatly paved and trimmed by the City Parks Department. We even patrolled the area by foot as much as we could, but we couldn't be everywhere, and some piece of puke took advantage of that and struck the lady.

Heather Allison was in her senior year at Pitt College, majoring in International Politics with a minor in Psychology. A vibrant young woman with a bright future and her whole life to be lived probably never gave it a second thought that some two-legged animal would be the instrument of her demise. The Coroner said her attack was swift, brutal and her final breaths were quick. We pulled up to the Montrose Towers and double parked right by the front door, but we were cops and could get away with that. Vinnie came out the passenger side and me the driver's. He walked over to the spiffy-looking doorman, flashed our shields and got the man's undivided attention.

"*Garson!*" Vinnie said. "You got a minute? We need some info."

"Sure, Officer. Whatever you need," the attendant said. He was a medium-size guy in his fifties dressed in the standard Doorman's uniform with the crisp, black tie and a Captain's hat pointed due north and arrow straight. "Let's sit over here. I need a smoke."

We did our intros, and as Mr. Gerald Zemelka lit his Marlboro and poured a coffee into his Thermos-brand insulated cup he schooled us as to the "skinny" of what was going on in the neighborhood. I followed Vinnie's lead in this, because he had an incredible talent for getting people to open up and talk, but finally we had to get down to business.

"That's good, that's good my friend. But what we're here for is to see if anybody saw anything out of the ordinary last Sunday morning. Say around two to maybe five a.m.?"

"Define ordinary. There's a lot of crazy shit happening in this neck of the woods nowadays. We got freaks-a-nature all over this place that time of night."

"Like somebody hearing a woman in distress, or screaming. You notice anything like that?"

"Naw, I didn't. But...ah, no...no...you guys'd never believe me if I told ya'."

"Try me," Vinnie said calmly. "I'm pretty gullible sometimes."

"Okay, but let me tell you two something upfront. I ain't the type of guy who spreads gossip around like some old Neighborhood Watch lady, but I'll damn sure listen—you know what I'm saying? Anyway, there's some construction dudes that are working the next building and...well...the company is having a rough time keeping a steady crew there."

"Why?" I asked. "Is the boss a prick?"

"Naw, Eddy's a good man. It's just that the guys up on the eighth floor are getting...spooked; for lack of a better word. It's more like they're gettin' the shit scared out of 'em, and more than once."

"What's got them rattled?" Vinnie asked.

"Because they say they keep hearing a woman screaming, and her voice trails off like she's running away. To tell you the truth—lean over here. I wanna take you into my confidence."

Vinnie and I leaned down and got close to Gerry like he was going to tell us a Pentagon secret.

"Two weeks ago—it was on a Friday—the main man came over here to have an inspection, so I said my hellos to him and his people then disappeared to have a smoke. Mr. Bellamy is one of those anti-smokin'-tobacco-Nazis that are trying to take over the world, so I had to sneak one in the alley over by that next building. All of a sudden—like outta nowhere—I hear this scream, like a shriek, coming from up above my head. I looked up and no shit there ain't nothing there but a few pigeons trying to take a dump on my hat. It got louder and louder and then I heard this unbelievable…"

The doorman stopped, poured another cup and then made the quickest one shot-out of a flask-move to "sweeten" his brew that I'd ever seen. He lit another smoke with a hand that shook so much I thought he might burn his nose.

"I heard—swear to God Almighty—a…splat…or something like a pumpkin hitting the concrete, and then it got real quiet. I gotta tell you gents that it was so scary that I had to put the big pucker on my arse to keep from messing my uniform pants."

"Would you show us?" I asked.

"Huh? What? Are you crazy? There's no friggin way I'm going back over there. Sorry, officers, I know you guys got a job to do but I didn't leave nothing over there but a whole bunch of ass gas when that happened. You understand?"

"Alright, Mr. Zemelka," Vinnie said as he stood and shook Gerry's hand. "You been a big help, so you're done now. By the way, what's the name of that skyscraper now?"

"What it's always been; the Century Building."

-2-

The Century Building was built in 1907 and was, at the time, one of the tallest buildings in Pittsburgh. The bottom to top was filled with offices from a local-now-defunct newspaper to top secret offices later during WWI and II. Now, all that was there were demolition crews gutting the whole place to make way for medium to upscale apartments in the future. The foreman was a middle-age man by the name of Edward Gavarkovich. He was tall, well-toned with thick black-rimmed glasses and wearing a sterling, white hardhat, which meant he didn't do a lick of work. He met us in the lobby amidst the dust, the drywall and the sounds of men "talking to" their work, which means they were swearing up a blue storm at difficult projects, and sometimes it worked. He took a second, looked up from his clipboard, and after he saw two "suits" coming at him he got real defensive.

"Wait a minute now," he said with a stutter. "Before you start your inspection I want you to know I fixed up the things the Feds said to do last week. Everything now is on the up and up."

"Rest your sphincter, pal, and check these out," Vinnie said with a wide grin.

We flashed our ID's at him and he relaxed a little.

"Sure, okay. What can I do for you two?" Eddy said in a now cooperative tone.

"We'd like to talk to any of your workers who might've been here last Sunday morning. Early, say after the bars let out."

"I had a drywall crew up one the sixth and seventh floor that late mudding walls on overtime about then."

"Why the OT?" I asked.

"Well…it's like this. We're running…behind a little right now and it has to get done by a certain date. You know, contract incentives and all that."

"How can you get behind on an inside job?" Vinnie asked.

"Complications, that's all," Eddy said as he wrote something on the clipboard.

Vinnie went into his act. "Well, it's like this. Me and Detective Johnson here are looking for some side work for the holidays and all that. We've both done a little sheetrock work in our time and maybe we could work a deal with you."

"What kind of deal?" Eddy asked, a little shocked.

"We only work on the eighth floor. It's our lucky zone, so to speak."

Now Vinnie had a B.A. in English with a Masters in Bullshit. That last statement made Eddy's head snap to attention real quick. Immediately he knew what Vin was getting to.

"To tell the truth, officers, if I thought you were serious I'd pay you both time and a half and bring you a lunch if you'd work that floor. I'm having…some trouble there."

"We heard," I said. "But, hey, you're a busy man. Here's my card. Tell those men we'd like to talk to them. Make sure you tell them that they're not in any trouble, but they might be able to tell us something. There was a woman murdered then just down the street on the bike trail. Anything they could conjure up would be helpful."

He took my card and said he'd see what he could. As we got into the car Vinnie said something I hadn't thought about.

"You know, kid, I got a bad feeling about that place. Maybe 'conjure up' is a bad way to put it."

-3-

Wednesday morning, no call. Just about the time Thursday afternoon came around, and me being ready to waltz back to 7th Street, I grabbed the receiver.

"Hello. Detective Johnson here. What's your problem?"

There was a pause, and then the unmistakable sound of labored and excitable breaths.

"Mr. Johnson, my name…is…well, let's just say I work at the Century project."

The troubled voice of a young man with doubt in his mind was evident. Reluctant witnesses are easy to read wherever you find them. I wondered how Vinnie would schmooze this kid.

"Okay, pal, a name's not important right now. What I'm wanting to know is if you and your friends heard anything out of the ordinary last Sunday morning when you were working. Like a woman screaming for help, not to be confused with the standard yelp you guy's been listening to off the eighth floor."

I slipped that last part in to see how he'd react. Maybe if he thought I was cool with the paranormal angle he might loosen up.

"…You know about that?"

"Yeah," I said as I leaned back in my chair. "And let me tell you, I believe you on this. There's a lot of strange stuff in this world that can't be explained so I'm open to it. Gimme your first name and you can call me Jake."

"It's Anthony. We didn't hear anyone crying for help but there is this guy that walks up and down the street all night long. He looks…cagey sometimes…like he ain't right in the head."

"Would you know him again if you saw him?" I asked.

"Yeah, no doubt in my mind," Anthony said with the first steady statement he'd made so far.

"Why are you so sure?"

"Because…he's my uncle."

What the hell do I do now? I thought. *I need to talk to Vinnie. It would be a sin not to use the Vin. Yet, I ought to be able to figure this out myself. I mean I've got to take the ball sometime. I wonder if she…would…naw, I can't ask her to do that. It would be like she was a secret agent again. Albert would kill me if he found out. But…I have to ask him.*

"Anthony, you still there?"

"Yeah, I'm listening."

"Have you ever heard of the Club 40?"

CHAPTER FOUR

PENDING CONSULTATIONS

"Yeah, I've heard something about it. Is it for real? I mean the football part?"

"Yes, it's real and very vivid," I said. "Do you know anything about the place?"

"No, that's all, but ain't that enough?"

It was evident that Anthony knew nothing about Yana, and that would be of tremendous help to my plan.

"That's all you'll need for a good night of fun. I tell you what, you sound like a hard working young man, why don't you show up about ten o'clock next Friday night? My brother will spot you one visit on the house and maybe another friend, if you bring one."

"Ah...Jake...I don't have any friends to speak of. I don't know who I'd bring."

"Bring your uncle, Anthony, and no one else."

"Wait a minute, Detective...sir. He can't find out I talked to you—I told you he was crazy! C'mon now, gimme a break."

I took a deep breath and then drew upon my years with Vinnie as my guide. What would he do in a situation like this? He would probably appeal to their sense of...decency maybe?

"Anthony, let me be honest with you. I can tell by your tone that you're a stand-up guy, and you and I both know the right thing has to be done here. I don't have your uncle pegged for this dirty deed but he **was** in the vicinity and that means I have to look at him strongly, if anything just to eliminate him as a suspect. There's a fifty-fifty chance we're both wrong about him. If you had a girlfriend who liked to ride her bike whenever she wants, wouldn't you do the same thing I want to do? Think about it."

"Well, yeah, you're right. But how you gonna keep this a secret?"

"That's my problem. Suffice it to say you and your uncle won't even know you're being observed. I promise you that with all my honor. And if this works out for the best you've got my card. If you ever need a favor—that I can legally provide—don't be afraid to ask. Deal?"

"Deal, sir."

"Okay. Just come in the front door and take an immediate right up the steps. Tell a guy named Albert that 'things have been arranged'. Make sure you say that exactly. Goodbye, my friend, until Friday."

We hung up with me being as confident as I could be that he'd show. If he chickened-out then I'd have to act. Now, all I had to do was convince my brother and sister-in-law to go along with this. It was time for me to get into my bag of Soft-n-Warm-n-Mushy (a.k.a. bullshit).

-2-

I told Vinnie I needed about an hour of "personal time" which is code for "I'm on a secret mission and you don't want to know". The police station we work out of is called Zone 3, and it takes about fifteen minutes to drive to the Strip from there. I parked my all-black-with black-wall tires-Ford LTD over by the produce docks and walked up to the Club. **Everyone** in this part of town knew a cop car when they saw one and I didn't want to draw any undue attention to my brother's place. How long Albert could keep his invention a secret was anybody's guess, but none of his steady patronage would rat him out. Albert made sure they all had a lot of fun and fond memories galore. I adjusted my look, put on my best conciliatory face and opened the door. Yana was sitting at her spot at the bar and engrossed in a book with two half-naked male and female characters on the cover in the "Damsel in Distress" look. She loved our romance novels, and I think the reason was that in Russia all two people do in a courtship was split a fifth of vodka, rub their bellies together and make little comrades.

At least that was what Vinnie told me, and I don't think the man would lie about it.

"Where's Al?" I asked

"Upstairs with his beloved machine; where he always is," Yana said without looking up.

That salutation told me a lot. Things weren't going well in Yanaland, but I was staying out of that. Meddling in married people's affairs is a no-win situation for anyone, especially a relative. I climbed the steps two at a time and found Al behind the bar doing some odds and ends. He was about six-foot two, muscled up from every morning at the gym with a little mousse slicking back his jet-black hair. He looked like he was in a pretty good mood and I hoped asking him to lose two grand on a hunch wouldn't trash his day, but I am his brother so I had to bring it up for a vote.

"Albert," I said with a note of respect. "Got a minute?"

"What's this 'Albert' shit? You only call me that when you need a favor or some cash. Just come out with it."

"Okay, I'll get right to the point," I answered with a tone of disrespect. In my America, the older brother busts the stones of the younger, not vice versa. I filled him in on the scam and he kept his trap shut till I was done. I told him I'd use the hidden staircase with the one-way mirror he had on the outside wall to observe the perp. Then I asked his permission to bring Yana on board. That struck a nerve.

"You want to do **what!?** You have got to be shittin' me. Use **my** wife to psycho-analyze some freak that may be a murderer? I'll give you three answers bro; no, hell no and oh hell no. You're outta your mind. Get outta here."

"Now chill. Please, look at this."

I pulled Heather's autopsy photos out and laid them on the bar. Al didn't want to look at them at first, but when I shot him my I-ain't-going-away-till-you-do look, he surveyed them left and right. He pursed his lips like he was going to say something but belayed it.

"You think your man did this?" he asked.

"I'm almost positive. It's a cop's gut feeling is all I can tell you, but if this guy is that dark," and I pointed to the deep, purple scar around her neck, "then I've got to rule him in or out. Yana can do that for me and every other woman in this part of the Burg if you'll let her."

"And if she does this then no one's the wiser? You guarantee that?"

"Absolutely. I would never put her in harm's way; you know that."

Albert put his chin in his right hand and scratched his cheek with a finger, like he was contemplating. "Alright, go clear it with her. When's this going down?"

"Friday night, about ten. They'll come in and the younger one will say 'things have been arranged'. Oh, one more thing."

"What could you possibly want now?"

"A waiter's uniform, if you have one my size."

"What are you going to do?" Al asked as he broke into a laugh. "Try and make an honest living for once?"

"Maybe. What—you don't want me to see how easy you got it here?"

"You'd pass out just watching me work. Okay, you can try it but the house gets all your tips, if you earn any."

"Agreed. Now I've got to downstairs and talk to the brains of this operation. Capiche?"

I walked away while getting in the last shot, which I usually did.

-3-

Yana was sitting at her barstool, checking out the three businessmen that'd just sat down. She studied them without blinking, looking up just long enough to assign them a number. I waited off to one side until she had given the order to their waiter and then made my approach. I knew I'd have to phrase this properly because she'd been manipulated by any number of devious people in her past, and I knew I wasn't one of them. Manipulators maneuver people into bending to their will by any…means…possible. Don't pay any attention to that last statement.

"Yana, dear, my most trusted friend. May we talk?" I said quietly as I sat beside her.

"Jacob, you have a much troubled look on your guilty face. Why do you try to…bullstein me—is that the proper word?"

"Close enough. Okay, I should've known better than to try to pull a fast one on you. I need a big favor in solving a very disturbing case and I believe, with your obvious talents, that you can help me make quick work of it."

I slid the same pics her way as I did Al. She looked at them quickly and then shoved them back.

"Fix me bourbon and water. And make one for you, too."

I complied with great ease and satisfaction. I knew she'd help me, but she'd want all the particulars. I sat back down, we took our opening swigs and she lit a cigarette. After a deep inhale I told her all that I knew; how Al said it was okay with him as long as she didn't get caught doing it and then I made my pitch.

"Here's the deal. I'm going to act as a waiter of yours. When they come in they'll go straight upstairs. I'll know them right away because they'll be way out of place there. Then you and I will go up the back stairs and hide behind the two-way mirror."

"What back stairs? A what kind of mirror? I know of no such things."

"Do you mean he's never told you about that? I mean you're psychic. How did that get past you?"

"Because material things do not interest me, for reading people and their personalities is my only gift. Albert must think it is not important for me to know these particulars and I will consult him later."

"Then you will help me?"

"Oh, of course. As long as I am not directly involved in any litigation or criminality."

"I give you my word. You will **never** be found out."

"It is settled then. Now I must climb the stairs and talk to **your** sibling concerning his lack in trust of me. You should—what do the Spaniards say?—vamoose?"

"Si. Until Friday…partner."

I exited like a bank robber who had just lost his mask. There was no way I wanted in that consultation, or intervention, however it works out.

CHAPTER FIVE

ASHES OF EVIDENCE

The rest of the week went smoothly with nothing more than B&E's (Breaking and Entering's) coming in to our zone plus a few domestic calls to visit and settle our way. I felt a little bad about not inviting Vinnie to my clandestine shindig, so I called him. He was at home, out on a sick day, when I told him about Plan A.

"Vinnie, I'm going to be at the Club Friday night and I was wondering if you'd like to join in. How 'bout it?"

"Wait a minute while I ask the boss. HEY BRANNA, CAN I GO TO THE CLUB WITH JAKEY FRIDAY NIGHT?" he asked and yelled.

There was this unmistakable sound of a wife-gone-pissed kind of silence that lasted about three seconds. Then I heard dishes being rattled together and what sounded like them being put in the dishwasher or one thrown at my buddy preceding some cupboard doors being slammed shut at warp speed. Instantly, I got her message.

"Ah...Jake, I'll take a rain check on this. My beloved just gave me "the look". You know what I'm saying here?"

"Gotcha. I'll get back to you Saturday."

-2-

Around eight-thirty I showed up to acquire my waiter threads and get mentally ready for the scam.

"Hey Yana," I asked. "Where do I get dressed?"

"In the back. See Roshandra. She will see to your fitting."

Oh shit, I thought. *Anybody but the "Sargent".*

Roshandra Harrison can be best described as a first-class, but very lovable, ball buster. She was tall, a little on the chubby side with jet-black hair, deep brown eyes and a model's eyelashes. She was the a-typical strong-willed, kick-ass, maybe take names kind of black woman and I found that a bit charming, but I didn't have to work for her full time either. Being Office Manager of the Year for someone someday, you work for her you walk the chalk or she'd cut your chalk line in a heartbeat. I presented myself to her for a fitting, but I wasn't quite fitting enough for her tastes.

"Jacob, when was the last time you met a Gillette twin-blade?" she asked as she laid a finger under her chin and tapped that effervescent foot of hers.

"I'm pretty sure it was Wednesday sometime. Why?"

"You know my standards here. Don't come looking for a job looking like that. Go back in my office, first drawer on the right, and get the electric razor. Go shave, clean your skinny ass up and we'll talk."

"Sure thing, Captain. But, being the nibby cop that I am, can I ask as to why a lady of your beauty and obvious virtue would need a razor?"

"Yes you may. Every once in a while one of these snotty college boys wants to look like a bum. They think it's fashionable but I don't. So, if they won't present themselves here properly I knock them down, sit on them and make 'em look good and I tell 'ya truly, it ain't pretty. You *do* wish to comply with my wants on this, don't you?"

"Yes, ma'am. Like it's my dying wish. By the way, I'm a thirty-two, thirty-four, if you have that size."

"The first is your waist size and the latter was your hat size, wasn't it?"

I walked away a little crooked, feeling something between my knees getting squeezed.

* * *

I did as directed, combed my hair and slid into my uniform of black pants, vest, white, long-sleeved shirt and a black, pre-tied bow tie. Rosh—who everyone called her behind her back—assigned tables one through five for me to clean and then seat the customers as they came in. Some smart-ass slob pulled me off to one side.

"Hey kid, is that broad at the bar the one everyone talks about?" he said, jovially, but I didn't smile.

"You mean the **lady** over there," I answered as I pointed her way.

"Yeah, yeah, that one. Is it true she can read minds?"

"If you're lucky enough to have one," I said with a cold, blank stare, but he didn't catch on.

"I'm gonna play a trick on her. When she brings my order I'm gonna tell everyone that ain't what I wanted. Won't that be a hoot?"

His second trimester-looking beer belly started to shake as he laughed out loud. I knew in a heartbeat how to handle this chump. I pulled him off to one side and flashed my badge.

"Here's the deal sir. I'm undercover trying to find a child molester that's been hanging around here the last few nights. He's a white male, approximately six feet tall, forty-five to fifty years of age with salt-n-pepper hair and who is seriously overweight. Have you, by chance, seen anyone tonight that fits that description?"

When the genius figured out I was talking about him or his double, his demeanor became extremely passive.

"No…no sir. I haven't."

"Oh well," I said as I offered him a handshake. "I took a shot, but thanks for your help anyway. Now, why don't you go sit with your family and enjoy what's brought to your table. And remember now—think pure thoughts. You never know who's listening."

He shook my hand and with a nod of his head he knew the shakedown was over. And I was thinking, *Hell's Bells, I don't need Vinnie now.*

I had arrived.

* * *

About ten after ten a young man came in the door with a sheepish-looking older man, and I instinctively knew my prey was here. They moved quickly up the steps and about halfway the kid had to coax the older one up. If that was my man, he'd picked up on something, and I was relieved when he made the climb. I immediately looked for the boss.

"Yana, I need to go upstairs now. I'll come get you when everything's in place. You still up for it?"

"Yes…I suppose. Are you sure I will not be discovered?"

"Don't worry. I've got it handled."

I only hoped that I did. I went to the back storeroom and was about to open the not-so-secret door when I thought of something.

How are you going to circulate right without being conspicuous? But… you are a waiter. Go get your tray and then reconnoiter the place.

Anthony and his uncle were standing in the back of the room, not knowing what to make of this scene. They looked at the magic box, the Dallas Cowboy Cheerleaders—who still looked double-damn good even at a foot tall—and both sidelines in utter amazement. My marks warmed up and came closer to the arena as we (Steelers) kicked off Super Bowl Ten. Albert walker over to them, Anthony pulled away from his uncle and, I assumed, mentioned the magic words. I saw Albert mouth "enjoy the show", meaning all was cool.

I approached a few of the other customers first, taking their drink orders. After three Miller's and two Iron City's I made my way over to Anthony. He was tall, skinny with poker straight blond hair wearing a lumberjack-type jacket and ten dollar jeans. He held himself with the confidence that any twenty-something virgin would and one tennis shoe was untied. I asked him what he wanted to drink.

"I'll have a Coke Classic if you've got it."

"Okay," I said. "How about your friend?"

His friend said nothing because he looked to be salivating over the cheerleaders; like I've got room to talk.

"Uncle Jack," Anthony said as he nudged his man in the arm. "Tell the man what you want to drink. I hear first round's on the house."

"Scotch-n-soda," he mumbled.

"Coming right up."

As I went down the steps I thought it was a good start. At least I had his first name.

* * *

I got the orders and delivered them like a pro. No one had really noticed me and that was a plus because I needed a little anonymity to take this to the next level. I stood back in the shadows and studied Uncle Jack. He seemed normal enough in his moderate dress and behavior but he seemed to…over enjoy the hard hits and especially the sack of Bradshaw on the ten yard line. When Franco extended a hand to his hurting quarterback, Jack's eyes seemed to shine and almost gleam as Terry walked away limping. Either he didn't like our players or he just enjoyed seeing someone in pain. Jack lit a cigar, a small Wild Cherry brand with the white, plastic tip. Every time he gazed at the cheerleaders I noticed a bit of drool coming from one side of his mouth. He was a sick bastard, no doubt about it now, but then a light bulb went off. If the spit did fit he'd never get an acquit. I dashed downstairs to make a phone call.

"Kevin," I asked softly, "this is Detective Johnson. Did I wake you?"

Kevin Thomas worked for the ME's (Medical Examiner) Office and was the best forensic man and lab rat in Western Pennsylvania. He was thirtyish, tall, almost gaunt in appearance and probably in bed by nine pm.

"Would it make any difference to you if I did?" he answered, just a tad disturbed.

"Not really, pal. I'm on the bike trail case and I need to know something. How long does it take to get back one of those DNA tests? I need one ASAP."

"Usually three to four weeks—why?"

"Can't we speed this up a little?" I asked.

"No, unless you pull some strings somewhere."

"Okay, I was just fishing anyway, but I do have one more question."

"Fire away. I'm the answer man," Kevin said with a hint of cockiness.

In real life most people need an "incentive" to help you out. I'd heard Kevin was a gambling man and I had a tip saved for Tommy the Hack, but nothing says I couldn't share.

"Kevin, you ever been to the Meadows?"

"I go there now and again."

"Then go Wednesday night. Third race, put all you dare on Tuckered Out."

"What's the odds," Kevin asked like a pro would.

"Nine to one. You won't be disappointed—ya' know?"

"Alright. This will be our little deal. Just you and me—no Vinnie. Bring the perp in and we'll swab him."

"…That might be a problem," I said, sheepishly.

"Why? Don't you have probable cause or something?"

"Oh, I've got cause, just not enough to do paperwork on. It's a long felonious story that you don't want to know. Bear with me on this, okay?"

There was a period of short silence, a sigh, and then a reply. "Whatever it is, make sure you stash it **immediately** in a sandwich bag; preferably one with a zip lock. Put it in a fridge somewhere and slip it to me in the morning. I'll see what I can do."

I thanked the man, and went straight down the steps to find a clean ashtray.

C 6

Yananna and the Magic Mirror

"I'm just about ready for you. C'mon, follow me." I said to Yana as I grabbed a clean ash tray.

We snuck into the backroom and up the secret stairway. Her eyes were wide open and bright, like she was Yananna Jones and had just found a lost tomb. As we climbed the last step and turned right towards the magic mirror she froze solid. I coaxed her over towards me, but she was slow and reluctant to answer my call. She was scared, and I felt low about it, but I had a job to do and I knew in my heart Heather's killer was in that room.

"Yana, please. They can't see or hear us. Just one look is all I need from you and we can call it quits."

She came to within an inch of the mirror and stared at the end of the arena facing us. Her bottom lip started to quiver, her left hand began to shake and then she stepped slowly back and pointed her left index finger straight at my mark standing at the south end zone, as plain as day.

"It is that man by the ashtray. He is a devil, but he is not what he appears to be. He is dark…and tormented….and very devious. Be careful with him Jacob. Be very careful, for his time is short."

Well, yeah, any murderer is devious, I thought, *but Pennsylvania doesn't have the death penalty now. Wonder what she's talking about? Now all I have to do is sneak away his DNA. I'll show him who's devious.*

"Alright, Yana, you did great. Let's go downstairs and have a vodka."
"Make mine two of them," she said.
"You mean a double?"
"Da."

* * *

Everybody in the place knew it was coming. I knew when Swanny caught that particular ball all eyes would be on him. Bradshaw dropped back, his line holding steady, and unleashed one for fifty-one yards. Dallas' Mark Washington was so close to Lynn that Swanny thought he was his whitey-tighties. Mark jumped up and caught the ball with one hand but it bounced, Swann juggled it and then made the "Catch" that's still a gem to NFL Films today. At that moment I leaned in between uncle and nephew to replace the dirty butt bowl and slipped in a new one. Everyone was so excited and high-fiving each other that it went unnoticed. I quickly went to the kitchen, found a Glad Bag and zipped this flimflam up.

-2-

The great thing about Albert's HoloBall is there are no commercials or half-time shows. He'll be in deep shit with the NFL if and when they find out, and there wasn't anything to be gained by pissing off everyone from the Budweiser to Butterfingers advertising people. By eleven the upstairs emptied; some went home and others came to the café for strong black coffee. I followed Uncle Jagov (Burg word for dumbass) and Anthony as they left for the parking area. They got in an old, Ford F-150—Jagov driving—and I got out my pen and pad to jot down the plate.

FIG 3668...hey, that's an Ohio plate. If the owner has a PA driver's license, he's mine.

I called dispatch and "Bad Attitude" Barbara answered. She was a short woman, cute, out-of-the-bottle red hair accompanied by a take-no-lip-from-you demeanor, but very smart and an ace at her profession.

"Barbie, I need a rush on an Ohio plate, FIG 3668. Can you help me? I'm standing outside freezing my jewels off here."

"Has anybody ever told you that you're beyond ignorance?" she asked with just a hint of sarcasm.

"Yeah, Branna. All the time, really. All kidding aside, can you hurry this?"

"Alright, as a favor to Vinnie. Let's see....it's registered to one Jack Morrel. Wait a minute, Jake, he's got a suspended Ohio driver's license."

"How long's he been here?"

"Ah…two years now."

I've got him.

"You want me to turn this over to Traffic Division?" she asked.

"Nah, I'll handle it. See if he has any known relatives in this area—pretty please?"

"Jacob, are your eyes brown?"

"No. blue."

"Well, they should be brown. You're full of shit up to your scalp."

"Is that why someone keeps leaving me forty-four ounce bottles of scope on my desk? Don't tell me I've got a breath issue."

"Ugh…you're hopeless. Okay, he's got a nephew. Name's Anthony Morrell. Does that help?"

"Oh yeah, sweetie. Next time I come in, what's the chances of you and me playing a little tongue hockey together some lonely night."

"Only if you buy a personality somewhere. Leave me alone and go do what the taxpayers pay you for."

"Okay, but one more thing, princess. You got an address on Jack?"

"Write this down 'cause I'm not talking to you for a while. 1103 Brinton Street, Swissvale. Bye."

When I retire I'm gonna write a book entitled *"How to piss off a woman in fifteen seconds or less."* I bet it's a best seller.

It was time to bring in the Vin.

-3-

With nothing much to do that Saturday, I dropped the DNA sample in Kevin's lab fridge and marked it "Mr. X". Vinnie was home, ready and waiting, to watch Penn State football. I felt the need to run some plans over with my mentor—Yana, the two-way mirror and the pirated DNA sample—so I thought it best to do it at his leisure over coffee. I called and forewarned Branna that I wanted to drop in for business purposes only and, after a land line cold shoulder and a disheartening little sigh, she "granted" me passage into her kingdom. I was so elated I almost dropped a log. We sat at the table in his storm-windowed-enclosed back porch with a table, chairs and comforted by a kerosene heater. This was Vinnie's smoking lounge.

"What's up, kid?" he asked as he lit a cigar and took a sip of expresso.

"I got a line on a suspect, and scarfed one of his slimy cigars for a DNA test."

"Is this one the up and up?" he asked as he took a long drag.

"You don't wanna know."

Vinnie had been "in the life" long enough to know when to quit asking his partner a question. The less I knew about his secret missions worked well for me if IA (Internal Affairs) ever called me in and it worked both ways.

"How we gonna get this one in for questioning?" he asked.

"That's where you come in, boss. I've got a cheap traffic charge but I don't know whether to play it yet."

"Is it something we can hold him on for twenty-four or more?"

"No…but maybe we can…invent something?" I asked with my eyebrows raised.

"When's the DNA paperwork comin' back?"

"I figure Wednesday or Thursday."

"How you getting it back so quick?"

"I got a guy."

"What the hell does that mean? I got a guy."

"You don't wanna know."

Vinnie gave me the "hairy eyeball" look that an old dude would cast at a young one. "Okay, Sherlock, I'll play this your way for a while. But, if it was me, I'd sit on the traffic charge thing until the blood test thing came back. Then we'll bring him in on the charge and first I'll go to work on him, loosen him up a little and then you go to work. Maybe we can scare him into giving us a swab voluntary-like. You got it in your gut that this guy's our man?"

"No doubt in my mind, partner."

"Alright then. It's a done deal. See you Monday."

-4-

There's never a dull moment in any big city and Pittsburgh was no different. Vinnie and me were called out at two a.m. Sunday to investigate a murder outside of a busy bar in the Strip, and it was a well-known hangout for ho's, pimps and druggies. The one under the white sheet was a drug dealer from the North Side and was "trespassing" in this neck of the woods. For this he paid his last dues, and with the corpse showing at least three bloody entrances, it was surprising how many people had a severe case of CRS (Can't Remember Shit). That's not a real condition, just something we cops came up with, but it seems we diagnose it daily. Bright and early Thursday morning I got the Kevin call and split for the lab.

"Did the tip pan out for you?" I asked.

"Yes, fabulously. Me and the misses are going to Cancun in February; thanks to you."

"Good deal," I said, cracking a grin. "Can you tell anything special by the results?"

"Only that it's male and pretty much contaminated. Get me a sample—a legal one this time—and I'll do it proper and pronto."

"Thanks, Kevin. You the man."

It was time to get Vinnie and drive to Swissvale.

-5-

A long, long time ago, way before football was invented, a shitload of people from Switzerland settled a town east of Pittsburgh; a shitload being 747 plus one more, if you have the room in the last wagon, which obviously they did. Normally it's a fifteen minute drive to Swissvale, but today there was the standard nine a.m. three-car wreck in the Squirrel Hill Tunnel. We pulled up to Jack's house about ten-thirty, and lo and behold, the Ohio-plated truck was in the driveway. I was the primary on this case so I knocked on the front door. He came to the door looking like death warmed over with a side order of dehydrated hangover.

"Jack Morrel?" I asked professionally.

"Who's asking?"

"Pittsburgh P. D." I answered quickly as we flashed our badges.

"Yeah, so? What you want? I ain't done nothing wrong."

How original on his part, I thought. *What a dickhead.*

"Oh no?" Vinnie said sharply as he moved confrontationally closer. "How 'bout the Buckeye plate on your rid and your driver's license? You been living here two years now. You too good to pay Pennsylvania tax or what?"

"I'll get around to it," Jack said, smartassily.

"Not good enough, sir," I said. "Why don't we go downtown and chat about it?"

"I ain't going nowhere!" Jack said, defiantly.

"Oh...yes you are," I said as I flipped him, put his head against the door—and I wasn't real gentle either—and Vinnie put the cuffs on him.

As we walked the scumbag back to our car, I had one dilemma. Should I warn him about hitting his head as he got in?

"Awh...shit...that hurt." Jack yelled.

Every man should know his limitations.

C 7

Hurricane Anthony

The traffic on the way back to Zone 3 was light now with everyone being at work or home from it. Jack sat in the back moaning and groaning about the headache he had that would turn into a brutality lawsuit later. Vinnie got this ornery-looking grin on his face and said:

"Hey, kid. Observe and learn. Jackie," he said as he turned to our perp. "Would you like a few aspirin?"

"Yeah. That might help."

"Okay. I've got three Bayer in my pocket. Sell 'em to you, five dollars apiece. How' bout that deal?"

I reached for the rear view mirror and dropped it to see Jack's reaction, and he wasn't a bit impressed.

"**Fuck you!**" he yelled.

Nonchalantly, Vinnie answered.

"Eventually, my friend, I probably will. But I must warn you. We at Zone 3 sprinkle sand in the KY Jelly too, just for your comfort—*NOW* shut the hell up and enjoy the ride."

I called Dispatch and requested all available info on our suspect, and then things got real peaceful for some strange reason.

-2-

Interview Room Number 7 had always been a lucky one for Vinnie, and by chance it was open. We sat a very quiet Jack down at the table, uncuffed him and walked out to let him stew a while. Vinnie had his own way to start an interrogation, and first he would study the subject's body language and facial expressions they'd make while being all alone. My partner could study a man for five minutes and tell me everything I'd need to know when it was my turn to play "good cop". Only this time he seemed…perplexed, or off his game somewhat. He said nothing to me except, "I'm going in."

Vinnie sat across from Jack holding a plain, open-ended filing envelope that he'd stuffed with twenty or thirty blank pieces of plain paper to give the impression we had a book on this dude. Funny how that move perked suspects up thinking, *"What the hell? All that's about me?"* Vinnie sighed, rolled up his shirt sleeves and wiped his forehead with a hanky.

"Phew, Jack, I see here you ain't exactly been a model Ohio citizen. Drunk and Disorderly January, 1987…89…DUI in April 1992…lost your driver's license for a year and then you just vanished. What seems to be your problem?"

Jack looked down at his feet because his inquisitor was giving him a blank, eyes wide open, non-blinking stare that he knew he couldn't escape.

"Buckeye cops are a pain in the ass. Every time a man wants to have a little fun those assholes are standing right behind him ready to pounce. I ain't done nothing all that wrong."

"So, what you're telling me is that your snuck across our border in 1993 without the proper paperwork—like a valid driver's license—and breezed into my town. What's the deal here, pal? You think we Pennsylvania cops are a piece of cake?"

"No...no officer, nothing like that. It's just that I needed a change of scenery...that's all."

Vinnie was starting—or gave the appearance—that he was getting pissed and it backed Jack up a notch. He gave Jack another cold, hard stare and then broke it off. Vinnie had him by the short and curlies now and Jack knew who the boss there was, so Vinnie lightened it up.

"Alright, Mr. Morrel, let's move on. I can see and smell that you never jumped on the wagon when you flew into town, and there ain't no sheet on you here, so do you sober up after you go on a binge? I mean, how you managing that?"

"I take walks to get my mind right first."

"And where's your favorite walking path at?"

"Along 7th Street."

Hot damn! I thought. *He's Vinnie's now.*

"Why that street?" Vinnie asked.

"It's a long story, officer."

"Then enlighten me. I got all day."

"Okay. I wet my whistle down on the Strip at Abe's place; right next to Feingold's Department store—you know where that's at?"

"Yeah. I know every square inch of this town. Please, continue."

"Anyway, when I get my fill and start seeing two moons I walk up and down that street to go see my nephew. He works nights at that Century Building project. He gets me a coffee or two and then I walk back to the bar. Ya' know, I'm his favorite uncle, and he'll tell you that too. He always has tried to look out for me. The night air and the exercise gets me home in one piece with no trouble with you people...not to say you're trouble, but you know what I mean...don't ya'?"

"So tell me, Jack. You ever notice the bike path that runs alongside 7th street?" Vinnie asked.

"Yeah, I know of it. I used to walk it too until some uppity little broad ran me off."

"Why'd she do that?"

"I dunno. She'd ride by looking all professional with the kneepads and one of those ugly-ass helmets yelling at me. She'd say 'Hey, this is for bicycles, not you alkeys.' I suppose she meant alcoholics. Then one time she rode right at me and tried to run me off the path. That's when I got real pissed."

Vinnie leaned forward slowly like he wanted Jack to take him into his confidence. "What do you mean by that, Jack?"

"I mean I went and told my nephew about it. I didn't want him to do nothin' about it. I just wanted to spout off."

"What's your nephew's name?"

"Tony; Anthony Morrell, just like my last name. He's my kid brother's boy."

"You remember anything about this girl, Jack? Like her height, race, hair color or anything that might help me?"

"She was white…had blond hair coming outta that helmet…and a wise-ass mouth."

"How'd Anthony take it you being bossed around by someone younger than you?"

"Not too good. He got red-faced, looked pissed and then for some reason he chilled out real quick."

"Jack, I want you to listen real close now. Did Anthony say anything about it?"

"Nothing much. He just said he'd handle it and then we dropped the whole spiel. Matter of fact, I ain't seen her for a couple of weeks anyway so maybe she got the message."

"I'd be willing to bet good money on it," Vinnie said, calmly.

Vinnie leaned back in his chair, put his thumbs inside his trouser waistband and turned around to the two-way mirror. I interpreted the look he shot me as "I don't know, but I think something's wrong here." And I was feeling the same way too. Intuition was telling me that our suspect didn't show a lot of anger when he brought up the girl, like he just brushed it off. I felt the dire need to call my psychic consigliore.

* * *

"Hey Rosh," I said, all excited. "Let me talk to Yana. Tell her it can't wait."

"Whatever you say. Here she is."

"To whom is it I talk too?" Yana said in her usually murdered English dialect.

"It's Jake. I just wanted to tell you thanks for the help. I think we've got Heather's killer here at the station and the old man is just about to confess. I can feel it."

"Vhat? Vhat did you speak? Vhat is this old man thing? I do not comprehend you," she answered in a tone that set off an alarm in me.

"Yes you do. We've got the guy you picked out at the game the other night—remember? Vinnie's working the old boy over right now, but something doesn't feel right."

"Oh dear Lord, Jacob. There has been a terrible error here. It vas not the older one I sensed…but the younger. The tall, thin one with one shoelace untied. It was the younger one…are you still there?"

* * *

The phone fell out of my hand. I felt like I could throw up. My instincts—that I had grown too proud of—had failed me. I was so confident and so convinced that I was right on this I was blinded to any other possibility. I realized then that because I just didn't like Jack's attitude and sloppy mannerisms I made a quick assumption that he was guilty. I vowed to never make that mistake again and to do a double take when anybody tries to pin a crime on someone else. Yet, I never thought a family member would do something that dastardly. No wonder all the veteran cops grow cynical. It's an occupational hazard that I hope I never suffer from, but I know I will. I walked around to the interview room door all humbled out and knocked twice.

"Officer Falbo," I said. "Let's take a ride."

"Anything you say, partner."

-3-

The trip back to 7th Street was a quick and quiet one. I pulled in a spot half a block away from the Century Building because I didn't want to tip Anthony off. I wanted to totally surprise the douchebag, drill it into his perverted brain that he didn't fool us for long and make a swift but public arrest. We caught Eddy in the lobby again, mulling over a desk full of draftsman prints.

"Bossman," I said as we flashed our credentials. "Where's Anthony?"

"Up on the sixth floor patching some plaster. Why, you want me to get him."

"Nah. We'll take it from here. We're throwing a surprise party for him so keep still."

We took the freight elevator to the fifth floor and then snuck up the stairs to the sixth. We eased around, finding out who was where, and spied Anthony on a ladder slapping finishing mud on a ceiling joint. Vinnie and me stepped slowly and quietly until we were two feet from him.

"Anthony, it's time. You have to answer for Heather," I said in a tone as cold as the arse on an Eskimo well digger.

"I don't know no Heather. What are you talking about?" he said without looking down at us.

This was a signal to me and Vinnie; no elevated voice nor a sign of surprise. My partner started to move away from me as we were anticipating having to take him forcefully, but this prick was shrewd. Immediately he kicked the wooden step ladder with one foot and the top rung dropped straight down and hit Vinnie in the right kneecap. The kid must've known Taekwondo or some other slippery Chinese shit because—in midair, mind you—he flung a huge amount of drywall paste from the palette at me. Now picture this. Vinnie's on the floor, wincing in pain and calling Anthony seven different kinds of mofo's and I'm trying to get this white goop out of my eyes. Anthony's standing there laughing at us and then he started to run out the hallway. I got twenty percent, I think, vision in my right eye cleared so when I caught a glimpse of his left foot I did what any good cop would do; I tripped his skinny ass. There he went, flying asshole over tin cup—I have no idea what that means but my Grand Pap used to say that, and it seems to fit here—and banged his shoulder on something. I cleaned the rest of my eyes off and immediately thought if I catch him I'm gonna kick his ass so hard and so high that he'd have to take his shirt off to take a shit. He was laying there moaning and whining about a broken collarbone when I went to check on my partner. Vin was up and hobbling on that bum leg when his eyes got big and he pointed towards Tony Numbnuts.

"We got a runner, kid. Go get him. I'll call for backup—now go! **GO!**"

I caught a quick glimpse of Anthony hanging a right towards the elevator, running bent over, sideways with one shoulder hanging low and looking like Quasimodo. I remember thinking it'd be easy catching this gimp but then some more of that slime slipped off my hair and I'm looking for a clean hanky somewhere. When he saw me he forgot about the lift to freedom because I had the back stairs blocked, so he franticly started to run up the steps.

I'm really glad there wasn't one of those camcorder junkies around because this had to look comical. He's dragging up the steps, I'm hot in pursuit using my jacket for a rag to get this volcanic shit out of my eyes but never giving up the chase and knowing that later that day I was gonna give this little prick the cleaning bill for my ruined threads. We came to a big red and blue sign that read:

FLOOR 8. GO NO FURTHER. DANGER

I almost had him cornered when he saw the only open hallway and shot in there. I was winded, in pain and out of patience when I peeked around the corner, my service revolver in hand. The hall was long, around ten feet high with one big chandelier in the middle, two huge ceiling fans on each end and painted a pale shade of blue. All the doors were boarded up and the lone window was covered by a make-shift one of two-by-fours holding a double or maybe triple sheet of heavy plastic in place to keep out the elements I holstered my gun because I knew I wouldn't need it now.

"Why'd you kill her, Anthony? What did you gain by that?" I asked calmly.

"I killed her because…" and he started to sob, "…because she tried to hurt my Uncle Jack, that's why. **No one** does that to any of my family. I even tried to talk to her about it. I tried to take her out to dinner, but you know what she said?"

"No, Anthony. Tell me."

"She said 'The only way I'll go out with you is if you grow a better looking head'. Ain't nothin' in the book says I have to take that kind of shit from nobody. You see now why I did it?"

"No I don't! No one has that right. But, tell me this, Anthony. Why'd you give your uncle up if you're so protective of him?"

"Because...he...he hurt me bad when I was a boy. He messed with me and...touched me places, and he has to pay now too. Can't you just...walk away?"

"No pal, I can't. Listen up. You have the right to remain—" and then something happened that I'll never be able to explain. The best I can do is describe it the only way I know how, and hope you'll believe me.

At first all the little lights on the chandelier started to dim and then go out, dim and go out until they started to flash on and off so quickly it looked like an old disco party. Then the front fan started to turn slowly and then the back one began. Together they turned faster and faster until one hell of a wind was being created and you couldn't even see the blades moving they went that fast. All of a sudden—I swear—Anthony started to rise up...I mean...levitate-like until he was about a foot off the ground. I felt myself being drawn towards him so I dropped on the floor and braced both legs against the other wall and held on for dear life. Then we heard a sound so gruesome that his bladder let loose and I was thinking **Depends!** *Where are you when I might need you?*

It was the sound of a bell. Something like a Church bell but way different. Like...an End of Days kind of tone. Like a ...Bell from Hell. That's when I grabbed hold of my gun—for whatever stupid reason—and Anthony looked down at the puddle he'd created. The look he gave me was the most frightful and fearful face I had ever seen on a live person or corpse. Then something Yana said came quickly to mind.

Be careful with him, Jacob. Be very careful, for his time is short.

The wind grew like a storm brewing and Anthony's face began to quiver. It looked like he was fighting some unknown G-force and his hair started to be sucked back by the gale engulfing him. The noise was so intense that I heard my ears pop or it was the plastic sheeting that was being sucked in and out. All of a sudden he started to move backwards at an alarming rate. He yelled for me to "please...help me" but I was powerless to stop this paranormal nightmare we both found ourselves in. The last thing I remember before I blacked out was the loud bang of the plastic being split down the middle by Anthony's sudden and swift exit out into the bone-chilling Pittsburgh air, his screams of torment as they faded into every foot of freefall and the unmistakable sound of a "plump" as he hit the alley floor.

I felt sharp pains on my cheeks as I came to. Vinnie was slapping me, trying to bring me around.

"JACOB! JACOB!" he yelled. "Snap out of it, boy! What the hell just happened here? Where's Anthony?"

I couldn't speak. I tried. My mouth was wide open but the words wouldn't come. I pointed to the mangled storm window and all I could get out was "There". Vinnie looked out the window in disbelief. He shook his head back and forth, looked down again and walked back to me.

"Jacob Johnson, I gotta ask you this as your partner and your friend. Did you throw him out?"

I shook my head "no" several times. Vinnie nodded his head and I took it he believed me.

"Okay, kid, okay. Backup's coming and a bus (ambulance) too. You stay put till I get back, but I've…I've got to take this," he said calmly as he gently took the gun from my hand.

And as if things couldn't get any worse, I can't wait to tell you about the "curtains ripping" sound I heard and the thousands of small pieces of plaster hitting the walls.

CHAPTER EIGHT

BOOZE, LIES AND PLASTER TALES

I heard the first "pop" as I sat on the floor, knees up, my arms on top of them and my head hanging low. This was a construction site, and I didn't pay much attention to a little plaster falling until the first cracking noise came and then it started to repeat rapidly. I looked at the wall in front of me and saw—swear to the Almighty—a line...or something being formed. It resembled a straight scratch sometimes and then it'd crook to one side and then the other. The indents became more rapid and the small bits of sharp, sheet rock were flying everywhere. I shielded my face with my arms and for the life of me can't say why I didn't get up and run, but this was happening for a reason...I think. All of a sudden it stopped and I felt safe in rising and looking around. There were seven different fissures of irregular patterns staring at me. They looked like run-of-the-mill imperfections but the more I gazed the more I thought it was a...message maybe? I leaned against the other wall and sank to my rump.

This is all wrong, I thought. *This just doesn't happen in the real world. No one gets thrown out of a building by the wind in real life. Maybe in an old Twilight Zone episode, but not here in Pittsburgh. How can I explain this to Internal Affairs? There's no doubt they'll crawl up my ass and pitch a tent over this. I gotta get a lie ready, because they'll never believe the truth...and I don't even believe it myself.*

The roaring sounds of sirens and the ambulance coming closer quickly snapped me out of my coma. I stood, shook myself off and walked to the window. Below was a bloody mess called Anthony Morrel, a man deserving the death penalty but not this way. I asked myself the most important question of my career. *If he **was** a jumper, would I have tried to stop him?*

The truth is…I don't really know, and I should.

Two uniforms showed up, told me they had to tape the area off and I told them to "Do what you gotta do". As I walked down the steps I met someone who I knew I had to see, but was dreading it. He flashed his Internal Affairs ID at me, as if I didn't know him.

"Detective Johnson," Mr. Dennis McGlothlin said, "let's pick a good spot. You know I have some questions."

Dennis was a tall man, fiftyish, with gray but perfectly combed hair, a ruddy complexion and dressed "to the nines" with the buttoned-down white shirt, blue tie and wearing a gray, London Fog overcoat. His poker face emanated a no-bullshit attitude, as with everyone else in his department, and the whole "Rat Squad" was definitely not on my Christmas card list. We walked past the sixth floor and I caught a peek of one of the truth goons helping Vinnie up, and I knew they were going to separate us; as per regulations. Denny picked a room for me with a folding table and chairs set up as a half-assed lunch room.

"You know the drill, Detective," he said as we sat across from each other. His tone was deadpan, judgmental with a side of "I really don't want to be here". "Let's go over this, step by step, minute by minute," he said.

"First things first. Where's my partner now?"

"Officer Falbo is on his way to UPMC (hospital) to get checked out and photographed," he answered curtly. "Let's concentrate on your story, shall we?"

"Whatever gets you your jollies…sir."

He didn't take that comment well because you have to have a sense of humor to get it. In fact, to make it in IA you have to take a personality test first, and if you flunk, you're in.

"My 'jollies', as you so crudely put it, comes when I get bad cops off the force. Not to say you're dirty, but you do have a reputation—off-a-***cer!*** Do we have an understanding now?"

"Yeah, pretty much," I said, not yielding an inch.

"Good then. Now, let's hear your version of what happened on the eighth."

I didn't particularly care for his tone. "***Version my ass!***" I yelled. "What I'm about to tell you is the truth and the whole truth. Are you ready to dictate?"

"Fire away. I'm all fingers."

So I told him my story verbatim. I was specific about Anthony's Jujitsu attack, Vinnie's injury, how the joint compound messed up my vision and my "do". He was unimpressed.

"Alright, Jake, that's good. Now, you're on the eighth, where's Mr. Morrell?"

"I got him cornered in the hallway."

"Did you pull your weapon?"

"No. Not immediately."

"But you did draw your weapon."

"Yeah. When I saw he was going to jump, my first instinct was to shoot him in the leg. Just wing him, ya' know? I wanted that piece of shit to stand trial. But he was too quick and I didn't think he had the stones to do it anyway."

"Well, him flying out the window did save the taxpayers a lot of money. Wouldn't you agree?"

Oh, this creep is good, I thought.

"How the hell should I know, Denny? What do I look like? Some kind of an accountant?"

He began to retort when I heard someone entering the room. I looked behind me to see one of his people giving the crooked finger sign meaning they needed a sidebar.

"Don't move. I'll be right back," he said, but I took it as an order.

"No problem. McGlothlin. It'll be like you super glued my ass to this chair. How 'bout bringing me back a Mickey D's coffee while you're out; two creams, three sugars," I said with my best wise-ass smile.

He left and I was praying to God that Vinnie was saying the same thing I was, or close to it. After a few minutes Dennis came back, sat back down across from me and had this evil looking smile on his mug.

"So, it is your testimony that Mr. Morrell leapt from that window in an apparent suicide—is this your side of it?"

"Well, yeah. What would you call it?"

"I've got two eyewitnesses outside that swear he came out backwards and was screaming all the way down."

"So?"

"So people don't commit suicide jumping out backwards, that's what's so. And they usually don't make a sound. One person said it looked like he was thrown out. What do you think of that theory?"

"What do I look like, one of those Karl Wallenda people? You're asking me all this acrobatic bullshit and I can't answer your questions. It's way above my pay grade. Now," I said as I rose to leave, "I'm going 'cross town to see how my partner's doing. We're done here."

"For the time being, Detective. I'll be in touch."

I was done trading barbs with the idiot, so I let that one go. Driving over to the hospital my mind started to race a mile a minute.

I remember something about a screamer close to that building. Where did I hear it...was it Gerry the Doorman? He heard screams from that same alley. Nah, that's nothing. That's some of that Poltergeist shit. It only happens in the movies. But what about that cluster bombing of plaster I got hit with after Anthony flew out? That was for real...wasn't it?

Going across the 7th Street Bridge, Bad Attitude Barbara called telling me—in a rather orgasmic tone, I might add—that me and Vinnie were on desk duty till further notice. I parked in our reserved spot, slammed the car in park, and headed for the elevator. One more head shot came as I walked to the E-Room.

Should I tell Vinnie about this?

-2-

I found him in the Discharge waiting room, sitting in a chair, legs crossed and twiddling his thumbs. "Where you been?" he asked, as if he didn't know.

"Shaking McGlothlin. You know what a dick he is. It takes time."

"What's the word from Central?"

"We're off the A list and on the S list," I answered, and I think you know what the "S" stands for.

"I'm ravenous," Vinnie said as he got up. "Let's get something to eat."

Whenever he says "ravenous" he means Primanti's.

-3-

Joe Primanti was a world-class entrepreneur. Right after WW II he started an old-fashioned roach coach (lunch wagon) in the Strip District down by the docks and stuff. He catered mostly to truckers who were picking up and delivering and this hard working bunch of stand-up guys needed a good meal in a hurry. One day a "Bobby Big-Rigger" was in a rush and told Joey to throw the fries and cole slaw over the whole damn thing and the rest is culinary history in our part of the Commonwealth. Our favorite one is the original on 18th Street. We walked in after dark and the place was about half full. We sat in a booth and ordered our usual.

Vinnie got the Capicola and cheese, I ordered the Philly Steak and Cheese and we chased them down with an Iron City draft apiece. Vinnie chomped down on his like a man, I requested a fork so I could scoop up what fell out of my mouth and eat it later, considering it as dessert. It's a Pittsburgh thing, and you just have to be there.

Anyway, when I thought the time was right I laid the whole metaphysical story out to my partner; step by step, mystic shit and all. He seemed to take it well until I got to the part about the plaster incident and he slowly removed my beer stein from my reach.

"Kid, you been hitting this stuff all too hard lately. I know living by your lonesome without the benefit of a woman's charms can do strange things to the male species, but I'm thinking you been spanking it way too much in lieu of the real thing. I think it's affecting your eyesight, just the way your Grandma said it would."

That was excellent, I thought, but I had a comeback ready.

"I don't do that! That's for teenage boys and married men over the age of fifty. In all seriousness it **did** go down that way. If you don't believe me I can show you as soon as we get off desk duty."

"Why not right now?" Vinnie said as he poured the remains of my happy hour into his mug and drank it all.

"Because it's locked up tighter than a drum. It's a crime scene."

"The place has got back doors, don't it"

"It does."

"Well? So what?" Vinnie said with his eyebrows raised high.

"You know what this means?"

"Yeah. We gotta find Billy," Vinnie said as he grabbed the check.

CHAPTER NINE

WHO IS HERE?

Billy Bender is what's commonly referred to nowadays as a "computer geek", whatever that means. Yet, I expect there'll be a whole squadron of them running about town fixing this and that someday; electronically speaking. He hung exclusively at the 1821 Club which was a bar/hangout for kids under the legal drinking age; 18 to 21, hence the name. They served only soft drinks but every cop in the Burg knew they'd all slip the hard stuff in via a flask. If they got caught, and the "Pocketful of Joy" was painted black and gold, no one said a word.

We found "Sir William" upstairs in the computer room set aside for his types. He wore a checkered, red and black lumberjack-type coat, faded jeans with holes in them but long underwear peeking through here and there. His 1994 New Year's resolution was to comb his hair, but I think he reneged on that by the way he looked. His black framed, Coke-bottle type glasses were held in place by a sport strap around his ears that were in dire need of a shave.

"Billy, Billy, Billy," I said as I sat beside him. "It's been a long time since we conversed."

"Ain't been long enough, Johnson. Nowhere near," he answered as he gave me a shitty look.

"Now that's not real neighborly of you, Willy," Vinnie said as he slapped him on the shoulder. "After all the times me and Jake have bailed you out of trouble, and you talk to us like that? Shame, shame."

"I turned over a new leaf, flatfoot. I ain't nothing illegal for going on two, maybe three weeks now."

Vinnie got perturbed. He moved over to Billy's right side and before Billy could react Vinnie snatched up his beverage

"Well, well, genius, what do we have here?" Vinnie said as he looked the tall glass over. "You're what—nineteen now?"

"Twenty."

"Now I just bet this is not all Coca-Cola. How about I do a chemical analysis?"

Vinnie took a big swig of the boy's drink, smacked his lips and said:

"I'm guessing this is fifty percent Coke and fifty Mr. Beam. How close am I, wise guy?"

In case you haven't noticed, Vincent Falbo has the strongest immune system known to mankind.

"Not bad, Mr. DuPont. It's seventy-thirty in favor of Jim. You gonna bust me for that?"

"Not just yet," Vinnie said as he sat on the other side. "Jake, fill this one in."

After Billy became cooperative, I laid it out for him. I wanted to sneak in the Century Building without busting anything up and I needed a non-professional locksmith.

"What kind of security system do they have?" Billy asked me.

"Front door's one of those new-fangled electronic types with the key code stuff, but I'm bettin' the alley side isn't."

"Okay, wait till I get my satchel."

Committing a felony, and knowing you'll get away with it, can be a beautiful thing.

-2-

It was around ten in the evening when we pulled into the alley where Anthony's parachute failed to open and there was still a painted outline of his resting posture. What I didn't expect to see was a black-n-white cruiser sitting there with the parking lights on and the motor running. My headlights caught the silhouette of two uniforms sitting inside and I assumed they were sent there to keep the scene secure from vandals and cops like me. I looked at my partner.

"Sit tight," Vinnie said as he opened his door. "I got this."

Vinnie walked easily up to the car using his version of an unabashed "pimp walk" which was comical to watch but never to comment on. He pulled his coat collar up and put his Steeler's toboggan on to shield him from the cruel, Pittsburgh-in-January night air that announced itself to every loose cartilage in an old guy's body. After he tapped twice on the window the driver got out and they talked for a short time. Before I knew it the cruiser left and Vinnie got back in. I needn't say a word because I knew my man the Vin had just called in a favor, or a "marker" as he categorized it.

"Billy," Vinnie said. "You got all your shit in one sack?"

"All that I'll need. Where's the lock?"

We got out and walked up to a fire escape door about halfway across the building. Billy took his small flashlight out and spied the lock. He hung his head and shrugged his shoulders.

"Do you mean to tell me that two of the so-called Pittsburgh Finest drug me out here from my nice, warm spot for something you could do? I mean shiiiit."

My turn.

"Well, young man, I suppose you could take off and me and Vinnie will find a way. Yet…it is way below freezing tonight and—hey Vinnie, did you see that brass monkey back there on that last bridge?"

"You mean the one that was ball-less?" he said, right on cue.

"Yeah, that poor bastard. Wonder how he got that way?"

"I dunno. Maybe Billy here can walk back and ask him. Billy boy, you wanna take a stroll?"

Billy got the message. He shined the light on it again. "One of you give me a credit card."

"Don't you have one of your own?" I asked.

"Detective, check out my wardrobe. Does it even **look** like I have credit?"

He had a point. I gave him my Marathon card, numbers down of course. In seconds he had it open.

"You first, Jake," Vinnie said. "It's your party."

* * *

We took the stairs up in case Eddy the boss was working late and about floor six Vinnie started to hack so bad I thought he might cough up a testicle, but he was still walking straight, so we moved on. At the hallway in question I hesitated for a few seconds, knowing I had to relive the whole sordid day over. I crawled under the caution tape and held it up for my "posse". They seemed unimpressed, but I was breaking a sweat.

"How 'bout you two come look at this and tell me what you think," I requested.

They complied with Billy looking at it without blinking. Vinnie gave it a cop's look at the "knowns" but he didn't get it.

"Jake, I don't see nothin' out of the ordinary," Vinnie said.

Billy was a lot of things but close-minded wasn't one of them. I could tell by his intense gaze at the wall he was visualizing something we couldn't comprehend and then he turned to us and spoke calmly.

"They got any paint in this place?"

"I suppose. This is under construction," I said.

"Then let's go find some and hopefully a roller because I don't want to be here all night. Look for anything but this color blue."

We all walked three floors down and found the parts room. All the one gallon cans of paint had their lids hammered shut but I found a half-full five gallon bucket open.

"Billy, will white do?" I asked.

"Yeah, perfect. I'll grab these two clean rollers."

We started to roll the white with me on the left and Billy on the right. The cracks area was about six feet high and about as wide and we met in the middle. After we finished we stood back against the other wall and looked at the…thing we had created. Something biodegradable just got chilled in us, and it wasn't supper.

"**Who**…is here, Jake?" Billy asked in a high and squeaky voice.

"I don't know, Billy, but I think I know who can help."

"You," Vinnie said. "Start walking back down. Me and Jake'll catch up later."

After Billy was out of ear shot Vinnie paced back and forth, occasionally looking at our mystery message. He was measuring his words as he usually did when he was about to get deadly serious.

"Jacob, I gotta tell 'ya…I'm out of this now. I don't know what kind of occultist shit this is but I never signed on to be a Ghostbuster. My best advice to you now is, if you plan on involving Yana—which I know you are—you better run it by Albert first. You gotta bring him here and show him this. Maybe that might change his mind, but maybe not. I'll cover for you as best I can—deal?"

"Deal," I said as we shook hands on it.

I dropped Billy off at the 1821, Vinnie at our station then decided to call it a day, go home and get some sleep.

If I could.

-3-

Desk duty is the most boring thing a cop can do. Looking over your brothers-in-arms' reports: paperwork. Answering the phone and jotting things down to give to detectives still on the "go" list: more paperwork. Filing evidence in the proper space; paperwork out the yang. I counted the minutes until it was quitting time and shot out the back door as fast as I could.

I sat upstairs at the Club nursing a scotch-n-soda waiting for my brother to notice the mournful look on my face. I didn't speak, just stared into open space like a little-boy-lost hoping I could tug on his heart strings a while. It worked.

"Jake, what's up? You and Vinnie have a falling out or something?"

"Nah, nothing like that. We're cool, but I got a dilemma that only you can fix."

"Really? Let's go back in my office."

* * *

Albert's office was a spacious one with a huge, cherry-wood desk covered by ledgers galore. He was a businessman and it showed in his skills and the bottom line. He closed the door and sat in his spacious swivel chair. I sat directly across from him, thinking about how I'd start this.

"Brother, there is no easy way to do what I'm about to do. You do know now that your wife helped us solve a terrible murder, and in record time. So…I have one more task for her but I want your permission again, because this is a whole 'nother story."

"What's so different about this one?" he asked.

"Okay, bro. Here goes."

I presented my story straight up and what worried me is that he sat there expressionless. No facial tics or "Oh **hell** no" coming from the look he was giving me. After I told him the happenings of the night before I ended by saying, "I rest my case".

Albert looked like he had stopped breathing. I didn't know where to go now because I gave it my best shot and then finally he exhaled.

"Now let me get this straight," he said calmly as he rested his elbows on the desktop. "You want me to voluntarily put my wife in the same scenario as she was in while in Russia. Is this what you're asking of me?"

"Not really; this is different. She can say no—hell, you can say no way—and that's that. But…something happened on that floor to I…think it was a woman. Don't ask me how I know that. I can't explain it myself. Yet…it's real. I swear."

Little brother sat back in his chair and crossed one leg over another, all the while tapping that damn pen up and down on the hardwood. I sat it out—what could I do?

"All right. What time do you want to do this?"

"After you close tonight. Say…two or three?"

"I'll promise you this. I **will** run this by her. If you see us there then we're in. Notice I said WE. If we ain't there, then we ain't ever coming. Can you live with that?"

"The rest of my life if need be. I'll be on my way now."

We stood and I extended a hand for a shake. He looked at it, stalled, and then shook mine in his. All I have to do now is think of a Plan B if this fails.

There's this new piece of technology back at the station called a Data Base. Maybe I should learn to use it. Look in some old newspapers for anything concerning that building. What the hell, I am on desk duty. Might as well make good use of it.

CHAPTER TEN

FUN IN GERMANTOWN

About nine o'clock that night I strolled into the station and checked in with the desk sergeant; one Arnie Trouten. He was sixtyish, gray haired with an overabundance of donuts stashed behind his tie. My greeting was cordial and with respect, his was the standard as in "I'm two weeks from retirement. I didn't see you. Go do something, even if it's wrong". I complied.

When I was first forced to use a computer I was told to create a password, so I did. Two days later I was informed that "passwordmyass" was not at all acceptable for an officer of the law, so I changed it. It was time to buckle down and do it right.

Let's see, I thought. *Try Century Building...death...eighth floor...what do I do now? Oh yeah, this button called Enter. C'mon, c'mon...I thought these things were supposed to be so fast...wait a minute, what's this? Pittsburgh Post-Gazette...July 13th, 1949. I wonder if this means something.*

German War Bride Ends Life
In Leap Downtown

A despondent German wife of an ex-GI leaps eight floors to her death yesterday afternoon around three P.M. One witness, Margaret Brauer, said Eva Rinkes, the 23 year old, auburn haired former resident of Munich,

Germany was sad she left her homeland and married Charles Rinkes. She presumably was going to the Foreign Affairs Office on the eighth floor to seek passage back to Germany, but never made it. She allegedly went straight to the fire escape and leapt off backwards.

"I was outside," Mrs. Brauer said, "sneaking a cigarette when I heard this ungodly noise behind me and…I looked and…oh, sweet Jesus, that poor thing was laying there all surrounded by blood…I can't talk about it no more."

The Coroner's Office has ruled it a suicide but the lead Detective, Andrew Rochester, said the investigation is still open.

Maybe I should pay Mr. Rochester a visit soon…maybe right now. I'll see if I can squeeze anything out of Arnie.

* * *

"Hey Arnie," I said. "Do you remember a cop by the name of Andy Rochester?"

"Do I ever. Now that was one good Homicide ace, I'm tellin' ya'."

"Knew his stuff, huh?"

"Yes he did. Nothin' got by that guy, and he'd argue with the top brass all day long if he thought he was gettin' the short end of the stick."

"Is he still around?"

"I think so. Last time I heard he was over in Dormont at the Heartland Hills so-called retirement home."

"You don't think much of the place?" I asked.

"No, absolutely not. I think they're cruel."

"Why?"

"Because they tie the old boy up at nine o'clock every night because he's got that restless leg syndrome and he keeps falling out of bed. Now that just ain't right in my book."

"Mine neither. So it would be bad timing to go see him now?"

"Oh hell yes. Wait until tomorrow."

I decided to take his advice. I hadn't gotten a whole lot of sleep these past few days because my mind just wouldn't shut up about this case. I had a meeting in one hour and my eyelids were heavy so I got into my locked desk drawer and pulled out two, extra strength NoDoz. I washed them down with a half cup of late-night precinct coffee that was close to gelling. It was time to take a ride.

-2-

I arrived at the building about ten minutes early and used my credit card to slide through and open the simple, back door lock. All the construction workers were off for the rest of the week celebrating the Holidays with their loved ones, all except for the Morrell's, and who really cares about them now. Precisely at midnight I saw Albert's Beemer slide into an alley spot and he and Yana stood outside. I opened the door, thanked them for coming, and we took the elevator up to the eighth. I stood at the hallway, making sure nothing had been disturbed, and ushered them in. Albert came first and then Yana slid by him and went straight to the message. She studied it like a surgeon would, tracing slowly every line and word with her eyes and hands. She stood back and walked to the window where Anthony met his end and walked back to us.

"This comes from beyond the grave. A grave of many years past. I can tell you no more than that, Jacob, for my talents do not flow to this side of the universe. I am sorry."

"Yana, please try. All I need to know is if this…spirit—or whatever it is—if it has a gender. Can you sense anything male…or maybe female?"

"I vill see."

She stood motionless and erect in the middle of the hall. With her eyes closed tight and her arms tight to her sides she started to softly chant something in a language other than Russian, which I'd learned to recognize but not speak. Suddenly her hands started to quiver and her chants became quicker until I got a blood flow problem.

"Jake," Albert said as he put a death grip on my right arm. "Call this off *now!* I won't have her damaged in any way over this. Do it!"

Before I could yell she snapped out of the trance. Yana, visibly shaken, hurried to Albert's side and held her arm in his protective grip.

"It is a voman…and she is vexed. She needs justice and she has picked you to help her. You have no other choice but to accommodate her now, Jacob."

"Did you by chance…get a name?"

"No, but I know someone who can, if Albert will permit it."

"Are you talking about Moneka?" Albert asked.

"Yes, it is she."

All of a sudden I got a little giddy. "Can we go see her now?" I asked, almost stuttering.

"No. She is in meditation until the dawn. We will go on the morrow unless Albert…"

"All right, Yana," Albert said reluctantly. "Just this once."

"Good, good deal. What time can I pick you two up tomorrow?"

"You can pick Yana up at nine o'clock," Albert said.

"Ain't you coming along?" I asked.

"No. I'm not going nowhere near that witch. She's all yours, big bro."

We called it a day, I went home and crash I did.

-3-

Vinnie and me worked the dayshift that week; 8a.m. to 4 p.m. He was hard at work, behind the desk, and taking a call. He wrote something down on a scratch pad and hung up the phone.

"Jake, we're outta this hell hole for now. I.A. cleared us to hit the bricks. What're you into right now?"

"I got a line on the eighth floor thing. Yana and me are going to see someone special at nine. I might be onto a name."

"Of who?"

"The doorman's screamer."

"You ain't giving up on this, are you?"

"I can't, partner. Yana says those words scratched on the wall are from the world beyond. There's no way I can let this go. Hey, by the way, ain't Branna a strict Catholic?"

That made him look up immediately. "She is," he said, but a little guarded.

"I bet she knows how to deal with this kind of stuff. You know, all those ceremonies and such about the spirits."

Vinnie leaned back in his chair and took a deep breath. His look of utter amazement made me sit back a little and get ready for…something.

"Kid, where's your wheel barrel?"

"What wheel barrel?"

"The one you carry your balls around in. They must be the size of watermelons to think such a thing. If I went and told my Irish Catholic wife what you were about to do she would immediately go find a Priest and a Monsignor, grab you by both arms and exorcise your ass to Cleveland if not some place worse, however hard that would be to find. **Don't** even go there—okay?"

"Okay, okay. I get the message. Where you off to now?"

"Penn Avenue. Two druggies played Ok Corral down there this morning and both were good shots. Me and the Coroner are gonna check out their sheets and then I'm going over to Saint Michael's for a minute."

"For why?" I asked when I knew I shouldn't.

"To light a candle for ya'. You're gonna need some help."

-4-

"Where to?" I asked as I open the door for Yana.

"Deutschtown," she said as she buckled up.

"You mean East Allegheny?" which was another word for that place.

"Ah! Vhatsoever you vant to call it. You are the local here and you are so…Pittsburgh!"

"Thank you," I said with a slight air of utmost pride.

It took a half hour to get to the town whose name I still can't pronounce. Along the way Yana filled me in on her friend, Miss Moneka Schaepher, who was a fortune teller/spirit conjure-up-er/soothsayer and maybe even dragon slayer. Albert was right; she was a witch.

She lived in a modest, two story brick row house on the corner of a quiet neighborhood filled with the aromas of sauerkraut and slitchengubens; whatever that is. It was an eerie seven steps up to her front door and I did the knocking in case the knockee got turned into a toad just for bothering her this early in the morning. We could hear the unmistakable sound of old, hard soled shoes accompanied by the squeaky sound of an un-oiled walker over a hardwood floor. She was just what I expected.

"Hallo?" she said softly.

"Moneka, it is Yana. I am with friend. May we enter?"

"Ja, ja," she said as the door opened.

Miss Moneka was short, no more than five feet I'd say, eightyish, of medium build wearing a full-length, dark blue dress topped by a cream-colored blouse laced with purplish designs of some sort throughout. Her hair was long and looked dirty. Streaks of gray *were* here and there but not totally covering her lined, weathered and all-seeing face. Her eyes were the color blue that landscapes are painted from, but what chilled me to a dead stop was the way they permeated my whole essence in a flash of time. I was taken aback, as Old English would phrase it, and I felt a split second of fear, amazement and then comfort all at the same time. This lady meant me no harm as long as I didn't do anything to piss her off.

"Young man, come into my parlor," she said as she turned slowly. She scooted slowly towards the front room walking slightly bent over and I noticed the right shoe's heel was about four inches thicker than the left.

She's had Polio, suffering from Osteoporosis and I'm bothering this poor woman for anything? Can I back out now…or should I?

"Jacob, let us make her comfortable. You make fire. I vill make some strong tea."

Moneka sat at a card table covered with a large, white-laced cover with a pot of nearly dead flowers in the middle of the spread. They was a neat stack of dried, cherry wood in a rack by the hearth along with some kindling to start a comforting blaze. I started it quickly—which really surprised me—and helped pull an afghan over her frail shoulders, all the while trying my best to find a crystal ball somewhere.

"Danke, young man…thank you. My hired man brings me vood veekly, for a minimal cost."

You idiot, I chastised myself. *Quit thinking he must be short and named Igor. That's crude, but it's funny as hell. Try to sound German.*

"You are very…velcome, Frauline. Enjoy the…varmth."

Just in time to bail me out of my foreign policy snafu Yana came in with a tray of exquisite, stainless steel… "Te-a-rey". Blessed with social graces I ain't, but anyway there was the tea, the cups, the light, the sweet and us, so we drank up while Yana conversed with the Queen in German, I presumed. Finally, they grew strangely quiet, and looked right at me.

"Tell me, my son," Moneka said calmly. "Tell me all about yourself, your past endeavors and your future wants so I may be of service to you."

I thought, *I only want help in one way and then I ain't never gonna bother you ever again. You've got me...vexed.*

I took a long swig of the strongest brew I had ever drank, inhaled and exhaled deeply. I started with my life thus far as a policeman and my burning desire to become a Homicide Detective. I tried to impress her with my true desire to see to it that everyone who takes a life must be brought to justice in one form or another; in this life or the next. On these points I was very sincere and I could tell by the way she started to smile slightly that she picked up on that. I took a breather and looked at the fire. It needed another log, so I threw one in.

"And what mystery befuddles you now, Jacob?" Moneka asked as she folded her hands in her lap.

"Okay, Miss Schaepher, here goes. But, you must promise me that this goes no farther than this room. I could lose my job if it was found out. Are we on the same page here?"

She looked over at Yana with a questioning face, as if she needed an interpreter. Yana said something in a foreign tongue and Moneka nodded a yes.

I told her the whole story from start to finish; of the Bike Trail murder, the Morell's but leaving out the night of HoloBall. Being European, I assumed she only understood soccer, so there was no need to go there. Finally, after several pauses to catch my breath and phrase things right, I got to the eighth floor happenings, and told her all. I leaned back in my chair unbuttoned my coat and loosened my tie because it was getting real hot in there, or it was just me.

"So, this is where I'm at, ma'am. I think I know who she was—"

"Jacob, before we progress, how do you know this spirit's gender?" Moneka asked.

"...I don't really know. But...when the message was scribed on the wall I just...knew. I'm positive. It was a woman that was killed there. Yana even picked up on that. I can't explain it."

"Then allow me to. There are three types of people in this world. There are phychic senders, receivers and then the very few like me who are blessed with both talents. Yana and you are both receivers, and that is a good thing. Use it wisely. Now, please varm up your vehicle and I vill go there with you. This vintry air is so hard on my old bones. Ve will leave at your behest. Yana, vill you help me to dress properly?"

Yana rose, helped the old woman up and out of her chair and turned to me with a big smile on her lovely face. With one hand around the lady's waist she flashed me with the other—now visualize this—a straight and erect...middle finger.

"What's that supposed to mean?" I asked.

"I think it is the way you Americana's signal...okay...or good job. It is, is it not?"

"Not exactly. But, you get her ready. I'll teach you the right way later."

As I walked to the car it became obvious that Albert had never taught his wife Americana sign language. Maybe he doesn't want her that familiar with our sordid customs.

I think I'll belay that part of her schooling myself. Maybe Al's right on that, but it was sooooo cute.

C 11
Sudden Impact

Traffic in the Burg was still light so we made a quick trip. I pulled up to the front door to let the ladies out and noticed a slight obstacle. Eddy, the foreman, was still there wrapping up some odds and ends and I didn't expect any witnesses for this little party I'd planned. I told the women to stay there for a minute. I needed a quick way to scam the High Priestess in without any pain-in-the-ass questions from a civilian. The front door was locked so I knocked.

"Yes, Detective Johnson. What can I do for you? I thought the investigation was finished," Eddy asked, a little surprised.

"It is, for the most part, but I'm here on another matter. I got a strange but possibly fruitful request. Can I come in?"

"Sure. What's on your mind?"

Here goes.

"Eddy, you see that elderly lady sitting in the front seat over there?"

"Yeah."

"Well, I'm gonna take you into my confidence. That extremely rich woman's name is Moneka—are you ready for this?—MELLON."

Eddy looked over at her with a stunned expression. "Do you mean, **the Mellon family**?"

For those of you that don't know the Burg, the Mellon family owned almost all the banks in Pittsburgh and Western Pennsylvania for many years, and are still a giant force in the financial community to this day.

"One and the same." I said with the same amount of surety as every conman I'd ever arrested.

"What in the world does she want with this dump?"

"She's thinking about buying it for an investment. I dunno, I'm just a cog in the wheel here, but seeing as how she reads the papers cover to cover she knows about the eighth floor incident. Now, she's from Eastern Europe and is very suppositious. You know, vampires, werewolves, ghosts and all that happy horseshit. She wants to go up and check things out before she makes a decision. I suggest you stay here. The less you know about this the better for you. You know what I'm saying?"

"Yeah, I'm getting the picture. Bring them in and I'll go to lunch."

As I walked back to the car I knew I needed to give the ladies some further instructions. "Now, you two are officially members of the Mellon family. Just go with that until we leave. Trust me on this."

Moneka looked back at Yana. "Can we rely on this man?"

To my surprise, Yana was very honest. "Nyet (Russian for no). But let us proceed anyway."

I was hoping for something better than a .5 star rating on my confidence level, but it was too cold to argue about it.

* * *

Eddy watched them come in, they exchanged social "Hellos" and then he disappeared. With Moneka at the helm, we took a one and a half mile an hour tour of the lobby to the eighth floor. As the elevator door opened Moneka seemed eager to go but then she stopped. She looked up and to the right, in the direction of Anthony's last stand. She made the turn and stopped again. She began to quiver so much that the wooden trinkets in her hair were clicking against one another and then she settled and turned to me.

"Many years ago something very grave and evil happened upon this place. A voman who found herself in an impossible situation vas martyred here against her vill, and her trials cry out for justice. Who among you vill help this poor voman to find peace?"

Before I knew it I found four brilliant and searching eyes directed at me. I started this whole deal, so I surmised it was time to man-up.

"I guess…I will, if you show me the way."

Immediately I wished I could've grabbed those words and re-ate them, because I'm ready to act but if Count Dracula's Aunt here says anything remotely sounding like "Go to the Light; Go to the Light" then these ladies better get a cab home because I'm outta here.

"Are you sure?" Moneka asked.

"Yes…yes, I am ready to be taught. Will she talk to me?"

"Not directly, but she vill through me, for this is vhy I vas born. Come children, let us hold hands and make a circle."

As I took each one of their **very** warm hands in mine all my inner fright began to wither and the searching soul in me was actually looking forward to this opportunity. To commune or just plain find out something about a side of the Universe that many people don't believe exist fascinated me to no end. I found myself with a thousand bursting questions but nowhere to start. Then, I heard her hum.

It sounded like the gentle singing of a woman at work in a kitchen, or nursing her babies in a contented manner, or at a sewing machine making a dress for her daughter's first dance recital. As Moneka turned to me her facial features seemed to change. She looked…younger and vibrant; kinder and innocent.

"Jacob," she…it…somebody said. "Vill you seek my assassin?"

"Yes, I will…Eva."

She looked at me dead-on for a few seconds. I said nothing, wondering if I was entirely wrong about her.

"Ja, Jacob, I see you know of me. I did not commit suicide. I vould never do that; it is against my beliefs. Vill you find this man and bring him to bear his guilt?"

"If I can, Eva Rinkes. I will not rest until I do. I promise you this with all my convictions of being an officer of our laws."

"Then go to Rochester. He vill be of the utmost help to you. Ve will be in touch."

And with that, Moneka returned. She seemed drained and almost exhausted. Yana and me grabbed her by the arms to keep her from falling. She shook it off, straightened her clothes with a quick brush of both hands and started to move.

"Come, young ones. Ve are done here today. It has been sufficient."

As we hit the lobby Eddy was back from lunch. He looked at me and I shook my head.

"No sale. Sorry," I said, trying to look forlorn.

We took the old girl home, I made her a roaring fire and told her my plan. She said to consult her about it, especially if I ran into something I couldn't understand, which was pretty much everything about the Outer Limits. Yana and me exchanged some small talk about it on the ride back to the Strip, but she was as ignorant of these things as I was. I stuffed a Mickey D's # 3 to go down my neck and headed straight for Dormont.

-2-

When I parked in the Heartland Hills lot I thought it best to get a little background on Mr. Rochester, so I called dispatch and got—you guessed it—Bad Attitude Barbara.

"Barbie Doll," I said, trying my best to rile her up. "What can you tell me about one of our own? One Andrew Rochester, Detective, Homicide, retired."

"Let me see," she said as I heard computer keys clicking at warp speed. "By the way, hotshot. Have you ever considered a career as a radio talk show host?"

"Yeah. Once."

"Then **forgetaboutit.** Your people skills suck. Okay, here goes. Andrew Winston Rochester, born April 1, 1919. Came on the force, 1929. Forty years, Homicide. Highly decorated, retired with honors—something you'll never see—in 1969."

"Any cold cases?" I asked, figuring any retorts on her assessment of me would be fruitless.

"Just one. Want the details?"

"Nah. I've got them. Have a blessed day, sweetie."

"Bite me. Over and out."

As I walked to the front door I had a strange thought. *I think I'll ask her out someday. Maybe to a Tough Man Contest. Yeah, that'll work.*

* * *

I walked in, found the info desk and asked for his room number.

"Are you family?" a nurse asked.

"More or less," I answered as I flashed my credentials.

"Room 305. Hope you have an enjoyable visit, officer."

Judging from that comment I walked to the door and knocked softly.

"Who's there?" a gruff and grumpy voice commanded.

"Are you Andrew Rochester?"

"Who's asking?"

"Pittsburgh P.D. Can I have a moment or two?"

I heard the sound of someone slowly leaving an old, vinyl chair. After a few slipper-type shuffles he opened it. He was everything I imagined an old cop to be. Tall at one time, he stood slumped over a little resting his frail frame on an oak cane with a few notches on it. I decided not to ask. He was terribly thin, but not malnourished I'd say, wearing a ruffled long-sleeve, white shirt and gray "grandpa pants" that were pulled up almost to his man boobs and held there by a set of patriotic-painted suspenders. His deep-set, dark brown eyes went **straight** to mine and felt me out immediately.

"Let's see your ticket," he said.

I flashed him a badge and a smile.

"What can I do for you, Detective?"

"You can tell me what you know about Eva."

That got his eyes and the door to open wide. He pulled another vinyl chair over to his left, sat in his and signaled for me to join him. I took off my coat, pulled out a pad, pen and began.

"Detective Rochester, I'm working a cold case right now concerning a so-called suicide in 1949. I understand you were the lead on that case."

"I was. Let's go first name basis. Call me Andy."

"I'm Jake, or Jakey; whatever you'd prefer."

"You look like a Jake," he said as he extended a handshake, which I quickly accepted. "Watcha wanna know?"

"There's been an incident at the Century Building. Maybe a suicide; maybe not."

Andy's head snapped up so fast I thought I heard his neck pop. I knew I'd struck a nerve, but I let him speak first.

"That brings back a lot of memories. How much time you got to spare today, sonny boy?"

"As much as you need."

"All right, here goes. Back in July of '49 me and my partner, Willy Simpson, were working the old 7th Street Precinct. Its Zone 3 now, where you work. We gets a call about a leaper at the Century Building down the street and it looked like a routine suicide until we interview a witness."

"Excuse me a minute, Andy. Was it a Margaret Brauer?"

"Yeah. Three-Times Maggie is what we eventually called her."

"Why's that?"

"She was deafer than I am. Every question we had to ask three times until she heard it and then she said the woman sat on the rail and went back quietly. We didn't think much of it until we interviewed a doorman and a trucker who was close by. They said the poor girl came flying off that eighth floor fire escape screaming her lungs out. Now that just didn't seem right to us, so we ruled it inconclusive for the time being. It was going that route until our Captain got ahold of it and he called us off."

"What was his name?" I asked, as if I really needed to know.

"Can't say. He took the Big Dirt Nap about ten years back and it ain't mannerly to speak ill of the dead, but I think he had his reasons."

"Can you share that with me?"

"Yeah. But, Jake, you got to remember this was right after WW Two and there was a lot a bad feelings about foreigners back then, especially against Germans and Japs. The Captain's son was killed in the Battle of the Bulge and he had an intense hatred for the Krauts. When he found out the stiff was a German, and didn't like it here and wanted to go back, he said—and I quote—'Piss on her. The only good Hun is a dead one'. So it got ruled the way it got ruled but I didn't like it much, and I still don't today. What's got your ears itching about this?"

Should I tell him, I thought, *about the Twilight Zone shit?*

"Aaahhh…you wouldn't believe me if I told you."

"Try me, sonny. I've seen more strange stuff that you have."

"The Morrell kid? He went out the same way."

"Damn. Poor Eva's at it again. We gotta help her," Andy said calmly, shaking his head.

"Then…you know about the paranormal part?" I asked.

"Oh yeah. Been going on down there for years. Why do you think some corporation dropped that whole place like a used rubber and sold it off for cheap apartments? Look, let's go down to the dining hall and we can finish there. You look like you need a coffee and I need a quart of Ensure. I'm just a tad impacted."

And off we went. Me with the need for caffeine but not needing any more info on Andy's problem.

CHAPTER TWELVE

THE SUCCER BOWL

We sat in the spacious lounge set aside for residents and their visitors. It was clean—almost antiseptic—with padded chairs and armrests. I got my fix and a smiling nurse brought Andy his. After a few sips, I got down to business.

"Andy, how long has Eva been haunting that building?"

"I wouldn't say she was spookin' it, she just likes to let people know she's there."

"Like she did Anthony?"

"Oh hell yes. The guy was dirty, wasn't he? She took care of it. The scumbag got what he deserved."

I still wasn't getting the answers I came for, but maybe I needed to drag the details from Andy. There was a story here. He knew it, but seemed reluctant to let it go. I drew upon my days with Vin, the Master.

"So, my friend, what's the deal with Eva? Help me understand why someone would want to murder her."

"Okay, kiddo, you wanna know, I'll tell ya'. She was brought over here by the KGB. Now that's out-of-the-box my thinking, but I can put two and two together. You see, a farm boy from Ohio got stationed in Bavaria about six weeks after the war in Europe ended. He met a beautiful frau by the name of Eva Kaeppel, and the hayseed fell madly in love with her. His name was Charles Rinkes and he was told—all our troops were—never to fraternize with the locals, especially the women but he paid it no mind.

The only thing that died about Fascism was Adolf, and there were plenty of communists around to keep things stirred up for us. The way I got it figured poor Charley arranged to have her brought over after his stint with the intent to marry her. I traveled to the Buckeye—St Clairsville to be exact—and interviewed him on my own dime. It's a sad story."

I had him on a roll, so I kept digging. "How so?" I asked.

"Well, the kid met her at the Immigration Center after Ellis Island cleared her. According to him, she didn't even kiss him hello or nothin'. All she did was give him an address in Yonkers and said 'Take me there, Charles!' So, he was dumbfounded but he did what she said. When they got there she told him to take a walk and she went into this old dilapidated house with all the blinds pulled. A car pulled up, two goons got out and one of them showed Chucky a luger that he had hid in his belt loop. The poor guy didn't know whether to shit or go blind, so he sat there for two hours. When she came out he took her back to Ohio and set her up in his mother's house, then went and got plastered. It was a bad time for that household."

I was starting to get it. "Do you think that maybe she was a…spy?" I asked.

"No doubt in my mind. But…she soured on the notion, I'm thinking, and got homesick. Going back to the Germany wasn't in the game plan for her."

"So her contact here contacted her straight out the window?"

"That's what I say happened. She got caught up in something that didn't sit well with her after a while. She left Ohio, came up here and went to the Relocation Office to get passage back. That's when Gunther paid her a visit."

"Who?" I asked.

"I'll be back in a minute. I'm having one of those prostrate moments that you'll have some day," Andy said as he hobbled to the Men's Room.

And I was thinking, *Damn, this is getting good.*

* * *

"Aaahhh," Andy said with a sigh of relief as he sat. "Gunther Beckenbauer. I suppose you wanna hear about that piece of work?"

"Absolutely."

"Well, that commie asshole was Eva's handler, so to speak. We got a tip from the local FBI that he was operating in Western Pa, so we got a picture of him and put him on the watch list. He got spotted a few times here and there and I even eye-balled him a couple of times. I never said nothin' to him, just followed him and stared his Aryan ass down a time or two. Then, he just vanished."

"You still have the photo of him, by chance?" I asked.

"Yep. Gimme that briefcase."

Andy opened the lid, shuffled some papers around and handed me three sheets.

"Here's his U.S. history, citizenship papers—who knows why he got legal—and his mug shot, circa 1948."

"Officer Rochester, thanks a million," I said as I glanced over them. "You've been a big help. Can't thank you enough."

"Sonny, you think maybe he's still around? It's been what, forty-six years?"

"If he is, and I find him, how 'bout I see to it you get reactivated. Would that make you happy?"

His face, eyes and whole persona beamed with delight as he lit up. "**NO SHIT?** You can do that?"

"Not really, but I'll do it anyway. Who's that?"

"Watch your language, Andrew. We run a respectable place here," an old and stern-looking nurse yelled.

"Yes, ma'am. I'll be good. No need to break out the rubber hose… sweetie."

She gave him a look that could crack glass, and went about her business.

"I gotta ask you something Andy. Maybe this is too personal, but Arnie down at the station says they don't treat you so good here. Is that true?"

"They never used to. This quack who comes around says I got something called RLA…or RLS…or one those new-age bullshit syndromes. I guess I did look like I was dreaming about kicking somebody in the ass all night, and then I'd roll outta bed. But a new doc came in and fixed me right up with a new pill."

"What'd he give you?"

"Viagra."

"You said…what?"

"Viagra. It's a miracle drug, I tell ya'. They give me one every night with my nine o'clock meds and by ten I'm sawing logs. I dream about my Marie—God rest her soul—and then I get a helluva chubby. It acts like a kickstand on a bike. Roll to the left; stop. Roll to the right; stop. Ain't woke up smiling like I do now in years. So, if by chance you'd like to get me a present for my help, how 'bout a vintage Playboy. Preferably the one of Marilyn Monroe. Are you gettin' my drift?"

"I'll see what I can do, but you're a dirty old man, you know that?"

"Not really. I take a shower every day. Now, go on—git outta here and go do your job," he said with an ornery-ass grin.

* * *

As I sat in my car I thought I'd just met a **real character.** I only hoped that I'd be half as cool as that old dude when I got his age. Before I put the car in drive I knew something was bugging me. I pulled out the papers that Andy had given me and looked them over again. This picture of Gunther…I knew that face somehow. I couldn't remember where or when, but his profile—especially his eyes—was familiar. I knew right where to go to get an answer.

I needed to find Sanjay.

-2-

Sanjay Patel can best be described as thus; tall, wiry, brown hair and eyes, thick glasses, nervous, hyperactive, overactive, chain smoker, genius. As soon as this exchange student from India graduated from Pitt with a million honors we snatched him up with a salary and perk package that he couldn't refuse to keep him from going back the Bombay Way. Give this man a fingernail and a DNA profile and he'd build you a human being on fine Kodak paper. Walking into his lab was like hearing someone lofty saying, "Houston, we don't have a problem. The 'Jay' is on the job". If anyone could put four decades or more on a face, it was he, and right to work he went.

"What can you tell me about this man?" Sanjay asked.

"He's German, a one-time-maybe-still-is communist, nasty-ass disposition and a woman killer."

Jay lit another Marlboro and tried to find room for it in an ashtray so full it looked like the summit of Mt. Everest. "He's got serial killer eyes, I can tell you that much. I've seen plenty of those to know."

"Then don't change those. They still probably look the same."

He went to work make Gunther's nose longer, eyes baggier, his thin lips thinner, and the hair white. In the space of twenty seconds he printed me a pic that just plain chilled my shit.

"There he is. I guarantee he looks just that way, if he's still alive."

"Oh…he's still around."

"How you know? Have you spotted him?"

"Yeah. The night of December 23rd. I'll never forget him. I've got work to do and I owe you big time."

"Gimme a good word on a horse someday."

"Will do, my man, will do."

-3-

For a cold war spy, the doucebag wasn't hard to find. Gunther had left Visa trails all over town. With their help, I got his address and found—and was it a strange coincidence?—him living in East Allegheny too and not far from Moneka. Having gotten through all the Sci Fi stuff, I asked Vinnie to come aboard to help me plan a trap for Gunther. I told him about all the help Andy had provided and it turns out they went way back. I suggested a rendezvous with Andy and us over a few sour cream and chocolate donuts. Vinnie smacked his lips, grabbed his coat and we booked out the door.

When we went to Andy's room, Vinnie and he shook hands and exchanged a two-second manhug. When we mentioned donuts and coffee the old man put his coat, scarf, gloves and Steeler's toboggan on in Olympiad time. I don't care what planet you travel to, **nobody** beats Dunkin Donuts. We hit the one in Dormont proper on West Liberty Avenue, got regular coffees for us and a decaf for Andy. We munched on glazed, sour cream, cinnamon frosted and each had a double chocolate for desert. We were right for the flight after all that sugar, and I gave Andy a progress report and my dilemma.

"This Gunther is a pretty slick individual, ain't he?" I asked our mentor.

"Slicker than snot on a January doorknob, that one is."

"Well, I need a plan to flush him out. Get him somewhere where I can sic two very astute ladies on his ass and maybe convince him to give it up."

"Who might they be?" Vinnie asked.

I looked at the Vin, and then at Andy. "Should I bring him in?" I asked.

"Hey, it's your party, kiddo. You give your side and I'll tell him I'm on for the ride." Andy said, nonchalantly.

So we told my partner about Moneka the phychic and our trip, and what little involvement Yana had in this crazy affair. To my surprise, Vinnie didn't bat an eyelash.

"All right, I'm getting' it now. I don't understand it, I ain't never putting any of this on paper—that's not negotiable—but I'll help you two vampire slayers any way I can. Deal?"

"Deal." And we shook on it like three Masons ready to chain the Devil.

"Gentlemen, I just got a strange-ass thought. What would that French freak detective do in a situation like this?" Andy asked.

"You mean Hercule Poirot?" I asked.

"Yeah, that schlemiel."

"I believe he was Belgium," Vinnie interjected.

"Same difference. I could give a shit; he ain't American. Anyway, I'd say he'd get all these people in one room, surround him and harang him till I can arrest the prick—I'm still gonna do that, ain't I?"

"That's the plan," I said.

"You two come closer. I gotta git a little nibby." Andy said as he crooked a finger. We pulled our chairs up for the pow-wow.

"Jacob, rumor has it that your brother has got *some* attraction upstairs in his bar. Something not too many people know about. Are my sources correct?"

"You might be onto something," I said.

"Okay, I'm on a need to know here, but I'm good with that. Gunther had this second nephew, one Franz Beckenbauer, who was the star of the 1974 World Cup championship. The sure-legged little punk scored five goals—and that's a shitload in a soccer tournament—and Uncle Gunther was very proud of him. Now, if by chance that final game could be shown in a pint-sized full-length operation, and Gunther gets a flyer in his mailbox about Albert's first annual soccer night, I'd say he'd show for that, as long as the Russian is clean out of his sight. I mean, we don't wanna scare him off. I'm just throwin' that scenario out there, that's all."

Vinnie and I looked at each other in utter amazement. Once a good cop, always a good cop, and it was obvious that Detective Rochester's wheels never quit turning.

"I'll see what I can do, but I think it'll work."

"Good, let's go back to the home. It's almost time for my little blue pill. Does Vinnie know that story?"

"Not yet. Why don't you clue him in on the way over?"

Vinnie laughed three of the four miles back to the home after Andy told him about his meds activating his natural parking apparatus, and I'll admit it cracked me up too. As Vinnie and I went back to the station I was lost in thought.

"Kid, how you gonna get your brother to throw a soccer party. I'd say it'll go over like a chili fart in a church pew."

"I don't know, but let me think on it tonight."

Going home I knew I'd have to dig deep into the bowels of my Best Bullshit Bag to pull this off.

A First Annual Soccer Night party? **In Pittsburgh?** *There ain't no way.*

CHAPTER THIRTEEN

MONEY TALKS, THE OTHER STUFF WALKS

      aul Kearns was a schoolmate of mine. We both went to Swissvale High, played football together, but his mind and heart were in enterprises and investments. He'd become very rich and I thought it time I visited him at his luxurious office in the Pittsburgh Business District; a.k.a. the

Golden Triangle. Yet, it wasn't a social call altogether; I had an ulterior motive. To entice my brother into "donating" his upstairs business without turning a buck **was** a bit ballsy on my part, so I felt the need to provide him with a good incentive. In plain language, I'd scratch his back and maybe he'd scratch mine.

I took the elevator to the fifteenth floor and walked straight into his office. The receptionist was a pretty young lady in her middle twenties, I'd say, dressed in a very conservative dress and high heels. I gave her my name, but no badge, and asked to see her boss. She hit the intercom, announced me and Paul sounded happy as he told her to "Send him right in". He was short, well-toned, sporting a hundred dollar haircut and a five hundred dollar Italian suit. We shook hands, exchanged some small talk about the old days and then I got right to it.

"Paul," I said as I sat across from him and crossed my legs, "I need a favor. Not a big one, just something to help out a relative of mine who's— how should I say this? — fallen on hard times. He needs to make some quick cash, maybe get in on the ground floor of a new thing. Anything you could turn me onto would be of immense help."

Paul looked at me for a few seconds, trying to figure me out. Cops usually don't come around unless something was up, and I knew he'd be a little suspicious of me.

"Well, Jake...I'll be honest with you. There is something coming up, and I'm very confident it will pan out handsomely to those who get in on the ground floor...but I have to be careful with that information. I hope you understand."

"I understand perfectly, and I know it's in the 'insider trading' category. Am I getting warm?"

"Pretty much," he said.

"Well, let me tell you a story that a little bird laid on me the other day. Once upon a time a man named Joseph Enzata, who works for the Security and Exchanges Commission, was hanging around Zone 3 and allegedly your name was dropped not once, but twice. It might have a happy ending, but I'm not sure about that."

As quick as my eyes locked onto his, he dropped his gaze towards the floor. My friend was in trouble; he knew it, I knew it. The color quickly left him and I think most of his blood was in his shoes. He took a pencil, tapped and rotated it on his desk. He plain didn't know what to say next, but I did.

"Pauly, I don't know what you're into here and furthermore I don't really care. But something's up, and as one old friend to another I might be able to help, although I can promise you nothing. Understand?"

"Okay, Jake, I got it. Tell your people to buy up as much stock in something called Amazon.com. Have you heard of it?"

"Yeah. It's a river down south somewhere, ain't it?"

I finally got a chuckle out of him. "Yeah, way south. You'll be hearing a lot about it in the future. Is there anything else I can do for you?"

"Nah, that should do it." I offered him a goodbye handshake and when he accepted I placed my other hand over his, Mafia style. "Take care of yourself, Paul. Take care of your family. I'll be in touch when the time is right."

He gave me a "thank you" nod of the head and I left, all the while hoping he wasn't in too deep for me to help.

-2-

My next stop was Sanjay's office to have him help me with the flyer thing that I hoped would work. He always talked about computers and technology being the cure-all for the upcoming 21st Century. I like the 20th Century. I'm very happy here. I want to stay here. To hell with all these buttons. I told him to leave out a date and time as I wasn't sure of it yet and his copier coughed out five copies announcing the ruse in perfect format—whatever that is—and color.

"Is there anything else you need?" Jay asked.

"Yeah. To tell the truth, I need a tape of the 1974 World Cup Championship game. The one where Germany won. Can you do that?"

"Sure thing, Detective. I'll have it for you on floppy disc in about an hour."

"Floppy what? How 'bout something on…stable disc? I don't want nothin' that's jumps around my car. I'm into something real delicate here." And I was very serious in that request. Jay gave me a look that I interpreted as "Boy, you are ate up with dumbass" and maybe he was right, but that's beside the point.

"Don't worry about it, Jake. It'll be alright."

"Okay. I'll be back in a flash."

* * *

I went back to my desk and told Vinnie about the flyer, the floppy thing and the bullshit I had to go through to get it. He was unimpressed.

"Jake, you actually think this'll work?" Vinnie asked.

"I'm hoping, but I'm gonna need your help with a few things."

"Like what?"

How can I comfortably tell him what I need him to do? I thought, but then came up with the answer. *I can't.*

"Here's the deal. If I can get Gunther and a few other schmucks to watch this wussy game, when the time is right I want Moneka to enter and maybe smack his strudels."

"That's no biggie," Vinnie said. "You give me the signal and I'll get her up there."

"Well...it might not be that simple."

"How so?"

"Well...she has to use a walker, so you might have to...carry her up."

Vinnie gave me a cold, black stare that I knew he had to learn from Branna. "You have **got** to be shittin' me. You mean like **threshold** style? I ain't doin' it. No way!"

"Hey, hey. I ain't saying you have to kiss her or nothing like that. Just... guide her a little. C'mon, be a pal."

"I'll mull it over," he said without looking at me. "Any other crazy-ass requests?"

The day's rapport was pretty much shot, so I thought *might as well.*

"Glad you asked. I want to get Andy a little present and I don't know where to start."

"Got it covered. He told me about the skin magazine too."

"You know where to get one?" I asked.

"Yeah. My house."

"No...not you."

"Yeah, me. Just 'cause you can't seem to get a steady whiff don't mean all of us are monks. I got two of 'em in the garage."

"Does Branna know about them?" I asked, but somehow knowing the answer.

"Are you kidding!? If she knew she'd cut my tap and my Johnny off. You keep still. I'll handle the gratuities."

I showed him my imaginary "locking the lips" thing with my hand, and left well enough alone. Now for the hard part.

Brother Al.

-3-

There's one thing I know for sure about my little brother's personality; it peaks between the hours of ten p.m. and two a.m. That's a great timeframe for a bar owner, unless you have a sibling—as in myself—who will ask for one hundred percent of anything in the hopes of a fifty percent return, which is thirty percent more than most people ever receive if you do the math my way. Maybe if I hadn't convinced him for his first twelve years that mom and dad bought him off of gypsies down on the South Side our relationship wouldn't be so…tentative. But I thought, *oh well, what the hell*, and took a shot.

"The answer is NO! I don't care what it is my reply is nada, nein, nyet, and oh hell no. What can I get you to drink?" he stated.

I realized then I would have to change my game face when I came calling for an unreasonable favor, because my passive profile was definitely **not** making it. I sat, ordered a bourbon with a Bud Light back and stayed silent until I could come up with a sure-fire plan.

"Albert, how would you like to be able to buy Yana a new Bentley, if and when she ever learns how to drive?"

"Yeah, it'd be marvey. But, I'm a little strapped for cash right now, you know, donating my services for the betterment of your law and order and all that—you know what I mean?" Albert said with his eyes WIDE open.

There was a shot in there somewhere for moi, but I had it coming, so I took it with a half-a-grain of salt. "I feel your pain, my man, but I'm onto something stock market wise."

"What are you now, a financial wizard as well as a ghost buster?"

"Not hardly," I said humbly. "But, I got a guy in the Wall Street thing that gave me a good tip on a stock that will make some **serious** coins. You wanna head's up?"

He looked at me like…well, I don't know what the look was. I think it was a cross between "Hi, old buddy," and "Git the hell outta here". Whatever it was, it changed his tune a little.

"So what have I got to do to partake in this good fortune?" he asked.

"Nothing much. I just need to borrow this room for about an hour at your choosing. I guarantee it'll be worth your while, and I wouldn't lie to you about that…bro."

He stared at me while washing and drying some beer glasses. "Okay, what's the tip?"

I schooled him on the Amazon thing and turns out he'd heard about it before, but never acted on it.

"Next question, Sherlock. What are you gonna do here for a whole hour?"

"…Watch a soccer game."

Albert shook his head so fast and so hard I swear I heard his adenoids change sides. Before he could go medieval on my ass I told him the whole plan; start to expected finish. To my utter surprise, he consented, but just on the Tuesday night after New Year's Eve when it'd be dead in there anyway. As soon as I was done with my sales pitch I paid him for the booze, tipped him twenty percent and hurriedly left before he could change his mind.

Around midnight I quickly and quietly placed the five flyers, with the date and time set with a black magic marker, in Gunther's mailbox as well as his neighbors; two on each side. That, I hoped, would quell any suspicions he may have if he thought everybody in his hood got a copy. I went home, crawled into bed but sat up and did something I hadn't done in years. I am by no means a religious man—and nowhere near righteous—but I decided to humble out and ask God for His help in this. Only a Power higher than me could bring about the long-shot at justice I had planned. As soon as my head hit the pillow, I slept better than I had in years.

Tuesday, January 2nd, 1996 would be the best—or absolute worst—day of my life.

CHAPTER FOURTEEN

THE PLAY

The flyer announced game time for nine p.m. so I showed up at eight. I told Yana to stay in the kitchen and do her best to coordinate dinners from the porthole windows of the swinging doors. She said she'd do her best, but she spooked Gunther the first time he came and I didn't want that to happen again. After setting up a few chairs behind the magic two-way window in the hidden room I called Andy and arranged for Tommy "The Hack" to bring him around back later and I'd pick up the tab. Changing into my waiter's uniform, and checking my look in the mirror, I was being glad I'd showered and shaved beforehand so Rosh wouldn't ream my ass out again about "appearances".

Vinnie rolled into an alley parking spot with Moneka around nine. After a few minutes he walked in, looked the place over, spied me and came at a fast trot.

"How much longer do I have to entertain the soothsayer?" he asked, and he wasn't real nice about it.

"Just till Gunther shows. Why, do we have a problem?"

"Yeah, I'd say we got a problem. All the way over Mrs. Nostradamus over there keeps wanting to read my palm and she keeps grabbing for my hand. I ain't into this."

"Vinnie, I'm thinking the old girl is just horny, that's all. Slip her the tongue once and she'll settle down. Trust me."

If looks could kill, I would've been one dead dude. His retort was classic Vinnie.

"Kid, have you ever played North Side Charades?"

"Can't say that I have, but I know the drill."

"Okay. What's this?" he said as he held up two fingers.

"Two words."

"Correct." Next he tugged on his right earlobe.

"Sounds like?" I said.

And then my partner held up a long, knuckley and erect middle finger, and I knew what that sounded like.

"All right. Bring her into the kitchen. Yana'll take over until she needs transport. You still up for that—you promised."

I didn't get a verbal yes or no on that so I assumed he was still a go. I reached in my pocket and made sure that my walkie-talkie and Vinnie's were working properly, and left his presence.

* * *

I ran upstairs to find—guess who?—none other than Billy Bender helping Al set up the machine. Billy looked at me sheepishly and instantly I knew who the "secret partner" was, but decided not to mention it and file it away for further blackmail references; not against Albert, but Billy. The stage was set, the three judges in the "Pittsburgh Inquisition" as I penned it were munching away in the kitchen and waiting for the sacrificial commie, if he showed.

Nine o'clock; no German. Nine thirty; still as elusive as Mengele. At nine-fifty-five, the door opened. Gunther walked in, looked left and right and asked one of the waitresses where the game was. As she pointed up the steps I took a good look at this monster. He was of medium height, thin with a full head of brilliant, white hair. The cheekbones were high but sagging, face wrinkled and his eyes were a scary shade of light blue. He hobbled up the steps one at a time, never taking his shaking hand from the bannister. Generally I'd feel sorry for someone that decrypted, but tonight I could see him falling backwards and I wouldn't try to help him until the dust settled. And then I'd kick him in the ass first just to see if he was still breathing.

I just wasn't feeling the love.

I grabbed Yana and we went up the secret stairs to the hide-a-way. She had a little trouble looking at him, but then she fixed a stare his way. Her eyes got glassy, her normal smiling face went dark and when she started to quiver I touched her shoulder and asked her to sit. Present were the ghoul and five other men who obviously liked soccer. The game was just starting as Gunther stood on the…does soccer have yard lines? He stood at the field's halfway point and looked straight down at his nephew. Here now is my best rendition of the most boring sports event I ever did see, with the help of the only European I know.

Me: what are those guys doing now?

Yana: They are doing stretching exercises. Like you're futeball players do.

Me: You mean **foot**ball?

Yana: Vhatever. You Americana's are so hung up on pronunciations.

Me: Not really. We just demand you speak the Queen's English.

Yana: The queen of Prussia?

Me: Surely not. Who's who here?"

Yana: West Germany is wearing the white shirts, the Dutch are wearing orange.

Me: Which one is this Beckenbauer guy?

Yana: I believe he is number five.

I watched Franz closely as he and the others warmed up. The skinny little son of a Bolshevik ***did*** have a wicked right foot, and was kicking the ball better than half the distance of this familiar-looking field.

Me: How big is the field?

Yana: One hundred of your yards long by fifty yards wide—why do you Americans not use meters?

Me: We do. We put money in them everytime we park our cars. And that's as close as we're ever gonna get to anything metric. Wait a minute, what's he doing?

Gunther stepped forward—almost touching the players—bent down and was saying something to his holographic nephew. *This guy's nuttier than I thought.* I looked at Yana and she just rolled her eyes and shook her head.

"This vill not be that hard now, Jacob. He is on the path to a mental... putdown."

I grabbed my two-way communicator. "Camper one to Camper two. Do you copy?" I said.

"Yeah, yeah. Stop the NASA shit. What you want me to do?" Vinnie asked, sarcastically.

"Bring our people up now, but quietly."

"On our way...Captain."

The game started with a kickoff from the center line and they were eleven players on each team. I was sure that our football influenced their futeball and I'm sticking with that theory. They all wore shorts, short-sleeve shits, black knee-high socks and some kind of running footwear the NFL would call "seconds". Yet, they did move fast and sure, kicking that white and black-stripped ball all over the place. Back and forth they'd go, with number five always on the run trying to kick it into a big ass net that you could drive a car into. My eyes started to get heavy already because this game was ***riveting***, and I'm being a smartass here. Why would people stampede one another over something this boring? All of a sudden Franz had the ball again and went zigzagging from left to right, flying by the orange shirts so fast *I* had trouble seeing him. The ball went in the upper left corner as their goal tender took a dive but missed the ball better than the average Cleveland Browns' player, which reminded me of a joke Vinnie would tell.

Question: What do you do if you find a Cleveland Brown masturbating on your front porch?

Answer: Go to the True Value hardware store, buy two cans of Rustoleum, and then spray paint his dick black and gold. He will never beat it again.

Now, back to business.

As Gunther tried to jump up and down with joy, his feet never left the ground but his lips kept moving. He was spouting off in German to the other dudes and they looked at each other, made the assessment that he was crazy and moved to a neutral end zone. I looked over at the door to see Vinnie giving the "all's okay" sign with one hand and wiping the sweat from his brow with the other. I gathered by the look he gave me he had to carry her and I only hoped that she didn't fart all the way up. That'd be an unpardonable sin he could never forgive, but I'll worry about it later.

Me: Yana, what's going on now?

Yana: The Vikings have the ball now.

Me: You mean the Dutch?

Yana: Same difference, as you would say. Oh no, Johan Neeskens just scored.

About that time I heard some announcer yelling what sounded like "GGGGOOOOAAAALLLL!!" at the top of his lungs followed by an eardrum-busting roar from the imaginary crowd and I started looking for a bunch of Swedes to trample over. The score now was a whopping 1-1. Well, whoop-de-do. Someone give me a greasy bratwurst hoagie and a warm St Pauly's Girl to wash it down with.

As the Germans got the ball back it went back and forth; back and forth; again and again. Finally Franz got his mojo working and just kicked the shit out of that ball, dodging Dutch guys and leaving them with the facial expression "Where the hell did he go?" As Frankie-z got closer to the net Gunther started yelling again, moving his right hand in a "go, go, go" fashion as his boy slammed in the winning goal…and then the hammer fell.

"It's been a long time, Gunny," Andy said as he locked Gunther's hand in one end of a handcuff. "Fancy seeing you here. Hope you enjoyed the game 'cause it'll be your last if I have anything to do with it."

Gunther stood speechless as his fading memory tried to remember who had just accosted him. Somehow the game, the noise and the splendor of victory went silent. The room was still, teeth-clenching tense and after a few seconds of Andy's bone-chilling stare, Gunther looked down at the floor. Then something happened that none of us expected and even I, a hardened street cop, felt an armful of goose bumps coming on.

The sound of squeaky, walker wheels can be a chilling experience, especially when an eighty year-old woman starts singing in a twenty-something voice. She stood directly behind Gunther, leaning against her ride and standing as tall and proud as she could. The voice coming from her, as I remembered it, was definitely Eva, and Gunther knew it. Not only was his hand shaking but his whole rickety body as well.

"Deutschland, Deutschland über alles, Über alles in der Welt. Wenn es stets zu Schutz und Trutze Brüderlich zusammenhält." Moneka sang.

Me: What is she singing?"

Yana: It is Das Deutschlandlied, the German National Anthem.

Me: Can you translate?

Yana: Yes. Did you know I can speak six languages?

Me: I do now—c'mon, what's she saying?

Yana: She sings "Germany, Germany above all, above everything in the world. When always, for protection, we stand together as brothers."

My concentration on Moneka's performance was broken by the slumping over of Gunther as he comprehended the expedience of his impending judgment. At once my two, veteran partners grabbed him under each arm.

"***Stand up!***" Andy commanded.

"Yeah," Vinnie added. "Take it like a man, shitforbrains."

And our Pittsburgh opera continued.

"Deutsche Frauen, deutsche Treue, Deutscher Wein und deutscher Sang. Sollen in der Welt behalten. Ihren alten schönen Klang, Uns zu edler Tat begeistern. Unser ganzes Leben lang."

Me:...Well?

Yana: "German women, German loyalty, German wine and German song shall retain in the world to inspire us to noble deeds our whole life long. Unity, law and freedom with German wine and German song."

Me: Look! What's she doing now?

Yana: It is finished.

"***Vhy*** did you kill me, Gunther?" Moneka asked him at point blank eye range.

"Because! Because you did not fulfill your agreement. You would not do what you were commissioned to do for the Fatherland; the Fatherland. You were a traitor!"

Moneka's eyes grew a shade of black that wasn't invented yet, even by Crayola. No matter what your age or health, adrenaline can be a beautiful thing as exhibited by an enraged fortune teller who'd heard enough. With all the strength she could muster she laid a right hand slap across his face that landed so hard his false teeth went flying.

Then she shook her hand and uttered a few "ouch's" in German, I think.

"There you have it," Vinnie said as he cracked a smile. "What did Shakespeare say? *Chew upon that, asswipe!*"

The old gumdropper hung his head in shame, knowing his number was up. Andy got the last word in as he applied the other cuff, and I was sooooo glad I included him in this.

"Now, take this like a man. If you give me any lip I'm gonna take this cane and wear your ancient ass out with it. Gunther Beckenbauer, you have the right to remain silent..."

Everyone in that room was smiling, happy and proud of a job well done. Andy tried to high-five Moneka, but both their eyesight's were waning, and they missed. Vinnie turned towards the two-way mirror and gave me a blank stare. Then he smiled, held up both thumbs and I knew all was forgiven for the time being. I was smiling, Yana was ecstatic, and before I knew it we were giving each other a victory hug. Only...I held her close a little too long for her comfort, and she broke it cleanly, looked away from me and went down the steps. It was wrong; she knew it and so did I. I got in my car, took Moneka home while Vinnie and Andy took Gunther to the station. As I was driving to East Allegheny my mind went awhirl with crazy thoughts of what might be good for me in the future. I pulled into a 711, put the car in park and composed my thoughts as Moneka stared at me, not knowing what was going through my head.

"Moneka," I asked without looking at her. "What becomes of Eva now?"

"I do not know. Vhy do you ask?"

I slowly turned and blurted out my proposal for Eva and the future. She said not a judgmental word, but finally answered in a soft tone.

"If you insist."

Okay. It's time to go to 7th Street and visit someone who really didn't exist.

-2-

I parked in the alley, broke in the back of the Century Building and helped Moneka to the elevator. We were both quiet on the way up to her floor as there wasn't really much to talk about…yet. We got off at the eighth, and Moneka turned to me.

"My child," she said with sincerity. "Are you sure you vant to go through with this?"

"Yes, ma'am. I'm very sure. Let us proceed, shall we?"

We moved slowly to the Hallway of Fate, as I mentally called it, and I asked my spirit guide the all-important question. "Is she here?"

"Oh yes, she has never left since her last day. Vait here as I prepare."

Moneka closed her eyes and chanted something in a language I didn't understand. Her whole persona changed and I knew who she was.

"Eva, it is I, Jacob Johnson. You're killer is in custody and now justice will be served."

"I see this," Moneka/Eva said in a calm tone. "I vish to thank you, kind sir, for your endeavor in this matter. I am vell pleased."

"Now you can rest, my dear, for your tribulation is behind you." I said confidently.

"Rest vhere?" she asked.

"Why…wherever it is you could go. To your…home, I suppose."

"But I have no home. I vill stay here."

I was hoping she'd say that.

"But Eva, you can't stay here. There are many people here who need homes; homes they can afford. That's what is planned here, and they won't come if you're still here. Please, reconsider."

"Where vill I go?"

"Come…come live with me Eva Kaeppel. I am alone, and you will find comfort there. I promise."

After a long period of eerie silence, she answered.

"I vill ponder it. But as for today, depart from here for Moneka needs rest. I vill be in touch."

As quick as she came, she left. I put my hands on the old woman's shoulders, straightened her hat and scarf and took her home. I saw her to her favorite chair, fixed her a "spot" of good, strong tea and started a roaring fire. I thanked her more than once and left for my favorite watering hole.

-3-

Hap's Bar was two blocks from my place, and I needed to get on a good drunk but thank God first for my good fortune. I know; it don't make sense, but I was real thirsty. Michael Pappas, owner, was a jovial man in his fifties whose fair pricing and great Greek cuisine kept his place packed. He was happy all the time, and no wonder, hence the drinkery's name. He set me up with a bourbon and a beer back and I inhaled the next six rounds. I was proud of myself, somewhat, for how the last two cases panned out. About midnight I stumbled my way home and it only took four tries to climb the thirteen steps to my back door. I fumbled around with the keys and I suppose I looked like a vision-impaired turtle trying to fuck a football; it was a bad visual. After I opened the door the dim light from a forty-watt kitchen bulb lit my way good enough—

What the hell did I fall over? That end stand wasn't there this morning. Find the light, dummy.

I took a swipe at the light switch and missed it three times, so I decided to feel my way over and sit in my Lay-Z-Boy lounger, which turned out to be a big mistake. As I eased down I didn't remember the chair being that low to the ground until my ass hit the hardwood. That's when I decided to find the lights before I had to go on disability. As the ceiling light blasted into my drunk and swollen eyes I had to rub them three or four times before I could focus. Before me was somebody else's place, because it couldn't be mine. Everything was different. It was arranged properly, I think. All the chairs were situated around the sofa, with lamps on end stands—complete with those fancy Amish-made doilies underneath that I meant to put out two years ago—and the whole room was…clean. I mean no shit you could eat off the floors or maybe throw up on them because the booze and the new culture shock wasn't sitting well with me.

And then I looked on the mantle, and when I saw that face I knew who'd done all this. She **was** beautiful, and there was no wonder Charley fell under her spell.

As I sobered up in record time, one wild-ass thought came to mind. Now think about this.

With a psychic on one side of me and a ghost on the other, is there *any* crime in Pittsburgh I can't solve?

I vill be in touch.

www.ingramcontent.com/pod-product-compliance
Lightning Source LLC
Chambersburg PA
CBHW021450070526
44577CB00002B/333